FARTHER TRAVELER

R O N A L D O   V .   W I L S O N

FARTHER TRAVELER

Poetry, Prose, Other

Counterpath
Denver
2015

Counterpath
Denver, Colorado
www.counterpathpress.org

Library of Congress Cataloging in Publication Data

Wilson, Ronaldo V., author.
 [Works. Selections]
 Farther traveler : poetry, prose, other / Ronaldo V. Wilson.
   pages cm
 ISBN 978-1-933996-33-2 (pbk. : alk. paper)
 I. Title.
 PS3623.I58572A6 2014
  818'.6—dc23   2014034097

for my father, who was, and is

CONTENTS

SONNETS

PROSE

FORM

OTHER

MEMOIR

ACKNOWLEDGEMENTS

"Streaming," "Loss," "Dalliance," "Glutton," "Metrics," "Then," "Where," "Multiply," "Chair," "Song," "Baby," *1913: A Journal of Forms*, Issue 5, Spring 2011.

"Birthday in Dementia," "The Broken Picture Frame," *Zoland: An Annual of Poems, Translations and Interviews*, Vol. 4, Spring 2010.

"Self Portrait as Dig," "Self Portrait as Fly," "Skin," "Pest," *Nebu[lab]*, July 2010. http://www.iiav.nl/ezines//IAV_607294/IAV_607294_2010_4/Wilson_lab.pdf

"The Women's Prison," "The Men's Prison," "Addiction," *Arch Literary Journal*, Issue 3, February 2010.

"Diary in a Dissertation," *War Diaries*, Eds. Tisa Bryant and Ernest Hardy, Los Angeles: AIDS Project Los Angeles, 2010.

"Double Life, or Trees in the Forest," "Double Life in Desire," *Nebu[lab]*, July 2010. http://www.iiav.nl/ezines//IAV_607294/IAV_607294_2010_4/Wilson_lab.pdf

"Poetics in Dream Tracking," *Evening Will Come: A Monthly Journal of Poetics*, Ed. Joshua Marie Wilkinson, Issue 7, July 2011. http://www.thevolta.org/ewc7-rvwilson-p1.html

"Poetics in Red Wing," (Excerpt) *Angles of Ascent: A Norton Anthology of Contemporary African American Poetry*, Ed. Charles Henry Rowell, New York, NY: W.W. Norton, 2013.

"Poetics Statement in the Great American Grille," *PoetryNet.Org*, Poet of the Month, Ed. Terri Witek, January 2011. http://www.poetrynet.org/month/archive2/wilson/index.htm

"Poetics After This Question: How do we invent the language of racial identity—that is, not necessarily constructing the "scene of instruction" about race, but create the linguistic material of racial speech/

thought?" *The Racial Imaginary: Writers on Race in the Life of the Mind*, eds. Claudia Rankine, Beth Loffreda, and Max King Cap, Albany, NY: Fence Books, 2015. *Race and the Creative Imagination*, Ed. Claudia Rankine, March 2011. http://www.newmediapoets.com/claudia_rankine/open/rw.html

"Poetics in Delusion or After Bitterness," *Acts + Encounters*, University of California, Santa Cruz Poetry + Politics Imprint/Annex Series, *eohippus labs*, Winter, 2014.

"Bear Gulch Diptychs," *BathHouse Journal* 'Radicalism Part 2.,' Vol. 11.2, Spring 2014. http://bhjournal. net/11-2/ronaldo-wilson

"Post-Dissertation-Intervention (i.)," Poem-A-Day Series for the Academy of American Poets, Ed. Alex Dimitrov, January 16, 2013. http://www.poets.org/viewmedia.php/prmMID/23834

"Post-Dissertation-Intervention (ii.)," "For the Sky, in Which You Will One Day, Belong," *Callaloo*, Volume 36, Number 2, Spring 2013.

"Ant," "Threshold," "The Fuckers Left the Head," "Morning," "Fire," "Lovers," *Bombay Gin Journal*, Naropa University, Iss. 38 Vol. 1, Winter 2012.

"Threshold," *Limited Edition Broadside, the Poetry Program in the Department of Creative Writing at Columbia College Chicago*, Designed by Clifton Meador, and Letterpress printed by April Sheridan, Chicago, IL, April, 2014.

"Letters," *Lit*, Issue No. 21, Spring, 2012.

"Part One of the Anti-Memoir": 'Sea,' 'Lot,' 'Puget Sound,' 'Rape,' Special Issue on Sex and Sexuality. *Interim*, Ed. Claudia Keelan, Volume 30, Issue 1 & 2, 2013.

"Part One of the Anti-Memoir": 'The White Van,' 'The Belgians,' 'Laceration,' "The Unspoken Body Issue." *The Mission at Tenth Inter-Arts Journal*, Volume 4, 2013.

"Part One of the Anti-Memoir": 'Candy, Again,' *Queer Masculinities*, Belladonna Material Lives Chaplet Series # 149, Brooklyn, NY: Belladonna Collaborative, 2013.

"Part One of the Anti-Memoir": 'Block,' (Under the entry: *William Pope.L*), 'The Capture of Samantha Pham,' (Under the Entry: *Swindler*), *The Encyclopedia Project*, Vol. 3 L-Z, Eds. Tisa Bryant, Miranda Mellis, and Kate Schatz, Providence, RI: Encyclomedia, 2015.

Much gratitude to the artist residencies where many of these works first evolved, to include The Fine Arts Work Center in Provincetown, The Anderson Arts Colony, Kundiman Asian American Poetry Retreat, Yaddo Corporation, and the Djerassi Resident Artists Program.

Thanks also to the following academic institutions that allowed me the opportunity, time, space, and means to complete this book, to include The CUNY Graduate Center, Mount Holyoke College, and the University of California, Santa Cruz, and to the faculty and students at these places, who provided many opportunites for discussion, collegiality and reflection.

I am especially thankful to the many writers and artists who have participated in, engaged with, and encouraged the work and play in this book, namely: Black Took Collective (Dawn Lundy Martin, Duriel E. Harris), Meena Alexander, Eve Kosofsky Sedgwick, Wayne Koestenbaum, Michele Wallace, Barbara Christian, Claudia Rankine, Charles H. Rowell, Carl Pope, Torkwase Dyson, Myung Mi Kim, Rob Nadeau, Andy Fitch, R. Erica Doyle, Farid Matuk, Khary Polk, Tisa Bryant, John Keene, Joshua Marie Wilkinson, Tamiko Bayer, Frances Richard, Jonah Mixon-Webster, Christine Hume, Terri Witek, Michael Angelo Tata, giovanni singleton, Andrea Quaid, Krystal Languell, Carolyn Cooke, Randall Babtkis, Ruth Ellen Kocher, Erica Hunt, Tonya Foster, Jai Arun Ravine, Addie Tsai, Wesley Yu, Iyko Day, Nigel Alderman, Don Weber, Siraj Ahmed, Amy Martin, Anthony MacLaurin, Ben Doller, and Sandra Doller.

Thanks to my publishers Julie Carr and Tim Roberts of Counterpath for their inimitable generosity and deep support. Finally, I am forever grateful to my family, and to my Love, Dallas W. Bauman III., without whom this book would not have been possible.

Urine, dark in a pouch, bangs on the thigh,
tethered to a catheter. Root to the bladder.
The gash in the sack—
What will heal is not remembered.
For instance, when my Dad goes for a walk,
but for the undulating water—
It may as well be the sky.
Clouds boil under. The irises
shake in the head, his stomps
in the driveway after he nicks
the van to get gas, or when the glasses
collect on the dresser: *Where are they?*
Mucus, he blows into the steel sink.
The plaid couch, doily-draped,
but under this, it smells of faint shit,
and the tray table shakes. A backhand
on the Tennis Channel thwacks!
Matches recycle. His dentures, sucked clean,

left on the plate. I Jack Mehoff in the booth,
to turn a trick for $20 at the LUV Boutique,
bald, skinny, a grey chest hair mat, fake daddy,
not my Dad's soft skin. Was it the stress of never
spending, his records kept by hand? He fainted
on the service road. I make it all up, being spanked,
for being a bad boy, then finger-fucked,
ass up on the pleather couch-back,
lit up by the screen, small bulb, but thick
to the hay bail bush. White dick is far
from the black father, far from being locked
in the shed, or the screwdriver in the latch,
or from the brother who traps. But being
sandwiched between one mouth and another—
Pockets in the house, remember. Inside,
in the morning's record between the first
and second sleep: Marrow melts in the dish,
and the butter, rich in the silver tray,
where grilled oysters fight back as they're eaten.
Remember the split envelope and on it, cursive
in a wobbly hand: *FARTHER TRAVELER*.
I flew across a country, and kept on driving,
further than anyone to get to the family reunion,
which meant winning a $25.00 Safeway gift card,
and soon with this, fruit bought, or pie, soap,

chips, or Cheetos. The body of a plastic bag
I tie. It defeats the gull on the roof,
and my Mom, she misses her "Pops,"
gone to golf, diapers packed, pills in slots.
He wonders at what's left, driven to loss.
Drive to the 'hood Valero station,
wipe the nozzle handle, *Pig Sty Stop!*
Another dream of shit wrapped in medical gauze
on a trail, but still stepped in it.
To wake, hosing it off a brown boot, un-owned.
Lost in your own house, to be trapped in the alarm
blaring after the burned sausage. There's no fire,
but ADT Security calls. The codename: fused
birthdates. This, nor his mother's maiden name,
does he know? The lens stabilizer holds the body,
moving, in the frame's center. It also projects:
I'm goin' for my walk. Around the long blocks,
or waiting on the street, driving cap embedded
in the window's screen, the blurred shapes.
An infected eye still contracts.
Fraternity brothers, faces painted in purple,
and gold numbers on the backs of shaved heads
on BuzzFeed, leaping in the rain, won't bring him back.
Nor can rage, nor will wanting to take a dump up
in this airport wine bar. The battery is dead.

No appetite—To eat only by the clock.
The sink on one side is packed with plates,
and the other, is for spitting. Sponges buckle.
Where the dog smells, the carpet's ripped out,
new bathtubs, new sinks. A new floor.
What's remembered is lost in the firewood,
stacked against the house, and the stiff, dead, cat,
poisoned then trashed, and an owl waits each night,
for weeks on the mailbox, its head spun still—
My father, he does know: *I got a bad memory.*
I'm not doin' you any good am I?

MOVIE

If the terrain were familiar, the poem would be dead on birth.

STANLEY KUNITZ

In the film, *Inception*, anxiety causes the plugged-in-architect to be assaulted by strangers, first glares, intentional bumps, then all-out attacks—cars crash and buildings crumble to crush the dreamer.

Out of your senses, you escape across a bridge, sit groggily, coupled with your sister and a cousin, faceless, but you know it's your family, though white, at the base of a hill overlooking a flat lake.

Your black boots look long, and they're slippery, your feet wide. Blunt nose hairs sprout out of your ass crack. The geese bark as they head south in the middle of your construction, but you don't mark this, as awe.

You're late for an application to Williams—$56, Expressed down the drain, but one thing's for sure—you'll keep making work, and sucking dick, relentlessly, like the stinger pumping venom in the arm, even after the bee's torn off.

So tired of this SilverDaddies search—your dementia-father attacks his wife in the night, bursting awake: *You're the enemy! You're my wife?* In every act now, the mother, ripped from sleep, hides under her bed.

In his boxers, a blubbery white man, redhead with a beard, pubic-looking, slept in your mom's milk-blue Galaxie 500. He wanted change. You saw his pink balls. Your dad let him in—the stranger who was in your car was in your house.

Squeeze through a window, somewhere on a train to face a baby across the net. Hit a serve that curves out to the right, then kicks wide, left.

SilverDaddy who's not online, lives within a 50-mile radius, holds shackles out in one picture, reveals rope nubs hanging from a ceiling in another.

This triggers the dream of your brother lying on a bunk bed, wanting a 6 x 9 surface to write on, but he's writing on a much smaller card, the note your mother will be happy to get.

You want to get change so you can make a phone call, or do some laundry, but there's no one to reach, and your clothes, they stink in the bathroom all night,

and only stink less, when you awake.

All these white men, with permanent jobs, walk through the dream. They set up chairs, and they're calm. They don't face the threat of flock, nor ambush.

The serve's slow, but everyone knows you're good. And in the end, you too, know that getting better means you have to go up after the ball.

Use your arm like a hammer.

Look at what Serena does.

This is what your father taught, and you fly up in the air,

reach up, higher, snap your wrist.

When the baby pulls the diapers from the trash, and is about to throw them on the court, you realize, you need even more control.

This said, when he hit the steel fence in his van, my father may have concussed.

       Before the new neurologist, we didn't think he could hurt, ignored the air bag, deployed. He didn't look dazed in the bend of questions.

   That night, I had a date with a Daddy without a cell phone. No way to reach him, so we met another night, and I rubbed his large cock in his yellow MINI Cooper.

   Porno blondes on VHS, my mother records over.

The apple pies that made my father happy still do.

       My dementia-dad: his shame and mind and fat evaporate, wanting so bad, to recall, but in the end, his refrain: *I don' know, I don' know.*

In the bed a corner of your body,
as if the night, and like the sweat
of the wet crotch—

When I drive, barely looking over
the column,
one wrong turn into another,
I lie to myself, but you drive
past me.

The toll, for
this lie, is that the post office
exists after five.
It's what one may call,
cheating.

The pussy-ass, opening,
piston-in, used again,
used so much, but still,

I get gifted satin sheets.

I feel the chair.
It's painless,
one turn down Elm,
an unmarked street, what a jerk.

A rose, I buy one, for you,
and the cashier charges me
for six.
Stop smiling so hard, you liar.

GLUTTON

Donald Trump confirms, with Kelly Ripa, he paid Lady Gaga $3 million to sing at his daughter's wedding.
— *Live! With Regis and Kelly*

This is what they paid for. This is what they want.
— JIMMY CONNORS

The lady in yoga behind you says she wants to attack the food. You've become the body you've become and wanted, and then Terry says, I noticed you missed two moves. If you think of him like the imperfection in the world as a Persian rug, you'll be able to forget this. You never want to be white, but then, your feet want you to be white, thin like they look in the mirror. Puddle and pool, pile and pool, what does feckless mean? Is this what it means to be feeble? It's next to fecund, which is closer to feces, I think, but I have so much I want to say. I can't tell you what to do. Doing is what I can't tell you to say. Don't bother me. Leave me alone, so I can figure it out. My healthy-father's small hands are smaller than the loan officer's at The Bank of Alex Brown. Dad's been taken again, loaned money to Mark Fredrickson, who said he paid him back $18,000, but he lied, and now the IRS sends my lost-dad the bill. Get another lawyer for another lawyer. Go after him. Is it worth it? Does it merit combat? My stomach hurts. Half wheat, half white, Nine Grain, it's still bread. The oatmeal looks like gruel, but I eat it. I want to run this morning, even though it's cold, black and dark. Eat the bread. It's bad to want the bread. Xerox it, save it, before you lose the outline, beaming, leaking.

... but it does contain a vital difference—of intent and intensity.

—MARY OLIVER

You think it's so simple, one breath-lung full,
　　　the master's form, master me, nigga what?

　　　The thing about you, you're tied to beef tongue,
stupid, black this, paint my face, dummy, Duh.

Cavorting the tracks that lack invention,
the spent, spelt, milk, this line is out

　　　　　　to reach the inner ear, a cranky fungus
　　　in the afterbirth. The way I see life:

too many swing sets pop up gold lilacs,
　　　gazing in the field—old, gas lawnmowers.

I'm in a ghastly geezer mask at the Big Y.
　　　Did you swim in the water? Dawn's over

　　　it too, there's constancy, yes, flow vs. rhythm—
Bacterium, silt: but please, switch compression!

You should have never told them—it's not that kind of day.
Many nails
                need to be done. Hair out, hair did.

Many things need to be complete,
                     clap to be shared.

So, things that you need to do: T.T.D.
That's not done, and even paper shocks you to stupor:

The words are MAGIC MOUSED.
                 Typing into a Mac is like looking into milk.

To the right of the poems, a Terabyte drive,
        a large load of, empty: I lost my Time Machine

        to the sculptor, whoooooooo left his body in the terrarium,
        and wrapped himself in an 80's sailor's shirt,

got called Sephardic.

At Yaddo, from the edge of the ping-pong table, the name
caller pursues a degree, and looks like

he caught the bug—AIDS FACE. Such an able-ist, Ape-ist.
Soap tastes like
soap.

In my desk, my doctoral diploma, and in a closet
my Master's, and somewhere lost my AB. A book

project, too, my name with one prize, and in another, a book
got two, but I'm black & brown—

I got to get a post: *No, no bictim, aim he fo NO a ho[l]e.*

At the park down the street and around the corner where we play tennis, I once heard buffed, bearded James say he seduced a woman in the bathroom, hiked her dress up and did her on the counter. John Borden, at our house, sitting on our couch—his junk hangs out, and his wife Mary realizing we have no toilet paper, dips in her purse. Doody, their son, is dark and gangly, and he hits the tennis ball over the fence like it's a baseball.

My Dad thinks everyone has athletic talent, or at least he knows how to read a swing, and Doody's is across his body & I wonder about my dad's knife fights in Nam. He says it's easier to fight someone with a knife than someone without one, because you can focus on one point.

Sometimes, I think of my father's body, the raised mole on his back, or the way he says, *At the bottom of the sea*, when I ask where it is, or he asks me, *What are you thinking?*—when I stare into distance. He follows my mother in the store, and one day, he'll simply be lost around her garden.

There are no more tomatoes on the vine, and a part of me is leaving as I enter the abyss of what I want to say when I awake, as if something was pulled out of me, where the pressure is only released by chancing on a screen shot: *ROGER FEDERER, STRETCHED*. *Fed-Eh-Reh*, Dad says & he spelled Flour, FLOWER on the Tupperware.

When my father was a small boy, he hit a girl, got caught & was forced to stand in the corner, wearing a paper dress and a "Dunce" cap. Or the stolen bundle of aluminum, a ball he made from tearing all the material off the backside of gum wrappers, fashioning this into a sphere, until a boy snatched it: who stole it—Dad—was he a sculptor? Did he ever draw? Did he make shapes?

All I want is to be in shape, but I get my fat from you, Dad, and I suppose I get my movement from you too, but why am I writing about you as though you're dead, when you're not?

Banged by 29 men, and you wanted some of them,
the red-ape, monstrous heaving, then sleep,
to wake, to be that cum bucket, filled.
You travel with Frank.
Maybe you're trying to hold onto something
in that hall you turn down. Some metaphor a life
can't hold. Slip up. Your life is upside down,
or appearing as some self, crawling up a hill.
Who do you run from, a man you speak Spanish to,
up on the railing—He looks down—maybe
you'll see a movie tonight?
He tucks a mug into his pocket.
A spider's attached to you.
"It's been there all day." Frank says, "The tea is warm."
The lot is black, and there's no one there to see you.
Bob pulls his dick out in the dark, makes it look young.
Touched by a bowl of chili: You ask for bread, inhale it.
Your insurance rises—what has gone down—
the quality of your erections, and all you want is not just
to be fucked, but to connect. It's what you say, at least.

Thank you for writing to me. I want you to know that I love you for writing to me. That you requested an application buoys my efforts, and I wanted to let you know, confidentially of course, that my work has won another prize, and that I am so thrilled. But like one real wife of Orange County says, *Imagine if I were married? All the things I could do.* All the things I might say—imagine, I want to say that I love you, that I almost saw you with Ben and Sandra Doller in D.C., that I wanted to see you, Rae Armantrout, but I was hung over from drinking with Abe Smith—maybe you're still looking for a poetry candidate? All I want to do is to catch up. I want so bad to leave this straightjacket, fly into a place where I'm not a visitor, or left by the road, like the killed animal clipped by collision. All I want is to leave this all behind, work hard in the hot room, leave my sweat on the mat. All I want to say, and all I want to do, escape, forget, *don't forget me.*

Don't hire the mixed black,
who understands complications
and sees your simple ways.
Pure native, pure polyglot—
these men, so stable,
these women, so frayed.
Hold it down.
You're not a slave,
on slave wages.
You're not an up-and-coming
star. You're in the stratosphere.
Yell it to the raft.
You've made it from root to branch.
I don't care what it takes—
The miners, they're transparent,
dug from the earth,
and now, out of the shaft,
released from the tube
in dark glasses,
smelling like what they left
behind, down there.

Fred has MS and explains before he shoots in me, pulls my panties down and gets me pregnant, that the lining around his spine is compromised, though he's strong as a horse, because he eats right.

After which, I went to a class to discuss Myung Mi Kim's, *Commons.*

"Helmet and Pot," one turned over to make another, the other roped in by the pull of sense—Maybe I was writing about a dream, or maybe I thought about shape?

You can lose everything you know, as from the fish that squeezes out one thousand eggs, maybe only one grows up to swim back to lay more.

Bitch, you want to get seeded.
Where did I go today? What did I do today? I went to a Funeral? Is that right?
Oh boy! I get to play golf—Is that right?

Maybe in that class, I said something like high formalist, because I thought they might think her work low.
But, it's obviously not.

Add: at the Garden, I finally saw Serena up close.
Difference? (And my father taught me this before I
saw it.)

She gets down low to the ball, knees bent lower
than anyone, and hits through it, penetrating,
pushing her opponents back.

Bubbles would do for the un-birthdayed sibling.
Plastic serration lining the inside of the wand's loop,
thin film of soap, blown like dandelions. White seeds
feather in a field. My father floats in not knowing
how to steer the wheel away from the car
that crushed the suer's pelvis—
bone fractures in his body, as my sister and I
arrive at the scene, taking out the golf clubs, the mats,
the booze in the console, the urine bottle hooked
on the head rest: we stash and stack.

My father recedes into another dimension.
Sometimes he stops behind the kitchen wall
to stare. Blown like dandelions, white seeds feather
in a field. A formalist I know, says *Writing free verse
is like nailing Jell-O to a wall.*
A student says, *I don't get it*, after reading
"The Arsonist" by Oni Buchanan. Each poem, of the same title,
mirrors the next. Like heat circulating in what's evacuated—

I wish I could burn into my father's brain,
sear what clots his thoughts, a plaque.

Where my father stares, maybe wondering about Namenda
or golf, his walk, a swim, or his brother stacking wood
in a van that no longer exists, my mother,
who drove with me down Center Parkway, sits in the back
of the wreck to stay warm. If *Writing free verse
is like nailing Jell-O to a wall*, I've decided to call my father
to tell him about a student found in his dorm room, suicide-dead
with a bag over his head. My father, as though in rhyme,
says, *My memory is going*, to which he adds,
I wish you wouldn't have called to tell me that.

My father forgets a name, Shon,
my sister's sister,
not my brother's wife, *our sister*, whose name is Libby.

I want to remember my father's voice,
how he was as loud as he's now lost. My mother
tells me he was lost at 24-Hour Fitness: *Don, Don, Don.*

No one came. She went to the car. She went back to the pool.
She found him by the treadmill. I want to write of her endurance,
her Tae-Bo kicks slow, sharp—her core building to the tube's low hum.

What I can't recall is her saying something
I can't quite capture. Was it about a cake mixer, a run, the snow?
—Yes, it was about us sledding on a pan down a hill. She tells my father: *They had fun.*

When I heard *Dad-Gummit!* fly from the foyer to my bedroom,
I thought he'd fallen, but he stepped on the picture frame we bought
from the Salvation Army where we shopped for a fashion show.
Ajani, his granddaughter would wrap herself in green.
Her friend, Arizona, picked out a flag star-spangled dress.
My sister was too busy to call, so the show went on
as I would oversleep.
My father would miss it, too.
In the V.A. Clinic out at Mather, when he tells the staff
I will be a doctor soon, they ask him *what will be his specialty?*
Not that kind of doctor.
I didn't want them to do that.
The glass fragments the fake hardwood.
He's mad. I'm sad. How simple a task, broken by a misstep,
which is not like the life of the bug, he did not take.
I was just about to kill a bug,
and then I didn't.
Some form may come in returning to the insect's *release,*

or in saying, no one was cut, nothing had to be stitched.
I brought him the vacuum, and a wet cloth,
and then left. When I returned, downstairs for a snack,
the pictures of Ajani, Baby Donaldo, Libby, Ceonita and Little
Milic, taped on cardboard, behind no glass.

SONNETS

Riptide sucks the body down, at Playa
Marbella, lost in the topiary.
Deep in the wrought, you glut in the riot.
Release your triceps: *What are you feeling?*
Thick as the dry shit caked on your index
finger. Spy it—Sniff. You rot canola,
ground flax. Fecal fucker, prolapse. Such mess
in your gut, a helix in the echo
between rooms. Nothing is where inside you,
you've hooked in, digging out the toxic grain
bound in the body. You own no truth,
because you were owned. Not ancillary
statue, pigeoned: the wash, sweet foul in
shame holding the body's infinite skin.

Compound eyes divide, brick red, exhaustion.
Its meated want, it wants to vomit on
my clean fingers. Hovers in the cubby
at Kinko's 24 Hour—sleep draws.
Not today—you won't finish the sonnet.
A worker's song pierces the room's quiet.
Sleepy, too, its pitch tight strung in grommet
—no draft, no back up, no flood of event.
But a flash, a small brown man in Tevas—
Yellow pulses between head and desk, fly
on my hair, neck, peeking in the crevasse,
flying in there. Why are you? You are why
we see eye to eye, fly. You've flown up in
here, marked, and ready, too, at the basin.

The Geezer paste in the Red Wing Y whispers
Fielding poems in my ear. Queer men piled
on one other, at some mountain cliff's
drop. Down goes the 72-year-old white,
tazed on TV, at the side of the road
in Austin, Texas, zapped by cop, she squeals
like a hog, seared by hot iron stoke.
How smug, she reclines, for the YouTube's glean.
The law by her side—this Grandma pushes
the pig, screams: *Give me the fuckin' ticket!*
The bird moth's wing flops, the beetle crushed.
Its outer shell pulvers when my Puma tries to flick it.
Dead and dead, the bug, insignificant
spun in the porch web, the brown corpse trapped.

Bleach burns plaid. Vietnamese agile
men clean bats. Biohazards in attics,
ton of their guano, bag after bag fills,
like bee after bee pushing. Stings splinter
out of memory's flush, a queen hides in
between the ceiling, its workers and drones
flood one flat. I take a sip of Riesling.
At Yaddo, the bats fly in the bedrooms,
strafe by the eye-ear in sonar's silence.
I, too, grab a broom between sleep and speech,
In the suite, bat bit, a writer's crisis.
Vision: a wheel is sculptured to a desk,
in the hall, a napkin, roach crushed to death.

THE WOMEN'S PRISON

after art in process by Ellen Petraits

Saliva, oil, wax in hexagons—
Prisoners wear slippers, hopeless *Candies*,
caramel brown, crisscross over white socks.
You say, *I am a wasp without the P,*
and I think Protestant, but not Person.
Becoming in process—such is the risk—
six sides, your patterns accrete in hives drawn.
Ephemera: bubble wrap, envelope,
velum release, your ink roots to my jail.
No knife—All I have: paper and poems.
No Styrofoam—All I have, a fragile
idea, porous lesson for poets
who see art as Code: *You think we're dumb cons?*
We're the smart girls that happened to get caught.

Under a hood, the ignition wires
are wet, insulation shot to shit, start
up sluggish. At the table's end, Michael,
or quiet Dan, bald crown of hair, these bars,
I want to take him out of this prison.
Be his bitch, get trained by the talky
one who understands the definitions
of *lyric, time, prison*. These men make me
nervous. The most thug life of the bunch slips
me his poem, about being water
hose whipped, that his mother was also whipped.
He's shy but he reads: *My Mother loved her
boyfriend more than me*. His atrophied
bicep divides the detainee from free.

What you can't resist are the polar bears.
No matter the bulb unlit, and despite
the tile's design, tentacle rays glare.
This white apparition, a poltergeist
in your libido, a booth in St. Paul,
Minnesota. Daddy's in a Knicks Shirt.
Daddy dentures—it's his last avowal
in the Adult Emporium porn's burn
of dollar after dollar that slides in
the slot of your mouth. You possess a shark's
brain, wired to hunt. Even Cro-Magnon's
cock, the furry archaeological
balls you'd suck. Monster, please, get over it
the green pollen: it's in the blood you spit.

PROSE

. . . . I become identical with the artwork, and the sequence is shortened . . .

ADRIAN PIPER

THE FISH

Squid, when jigged, and pulled out of the water, blast their ink into the sky. After being devoured or maybe after escaping (the eye cannot tell escape from striped bass eating squid) their ink underwater appears orange, threads. The light from the dock's lamps make the bay look green. Something deep is cutting below. Such is the case of a friendship bound by the pull of addiction, each leaning to whatever it takes to fill. So how do I return to what I want to say: What were the shooters trying to erase—what were they trying to fill? *[TXT: Have a great run. It's beautiful out.]*[1] This is the case, when the body runs, moves across an abandoned plantation field to days of road and sun, to see a pink fat fag in D&G hater-blockers, or a fag in pink, or a fat pink fag in brown VANS—what's the difference: belt/ stripe/ shoe/ belt/ line? It's all in the voice, what it measures, and how the body sets an argument. My addiction, as in finding myself on my knees on the Route 91 rest stop = the "dead nigger" Hilton Als sees and I see, too, in *Without Sanctuary*,[2] roped to a tree and looking up from his knees, mouth and eyes bulleted into oblivion. *Lemme have it.* I am thinking of two things: how do I make the case that the visual field Barthes describes, the layering of two nuns juxtaposed against riflemen in Nicaragua, is as central as the locus I have been tending, a black body riddled with bullets, a sheaf of white streaks in sepia, trying to think about Als's slowing down time by way of imagining the family who returned, to "cut Mother or Cousin Down."[3]

1. Text message from the painter Rob Nadeau, Fine Arts Work Center in Provincetown, June 2008.
2. Hilton Als, *Without Sanctuary: Lynching Photography in America.* Ed. James Allen (Santa Fe: Twin Palm Publishers, 2000) 39.
3. Ibid. 43.

THE WAITING ROOM

In the dream, I recall looking down at a list of words that are blown up to size 14 font, that are 'posed to be poems. I have cut contact with my friends, especially my black ones; and at the heart of my project is to make sense of what it means to be a fragmented black, or to refigure the fragments while breaking apart, as in, dragged, pinched, probed, bulleted. On July 1st, 2008, a giant black woman lay dying on a floor in the Kings County Hospital. Dallas says she was there for 24 hours. Her body lay stretched out, her head and top torso stuck under the immobile seats. Steel Seat Brackets as Arms of Death, I say. The reporter with surveillance video to prove it points out: *Here, her body is convulsing, and here, she is dying.* What this has to do with my dissertation is that I need to make the final push. My dad is losing his memory. He does not remember much from the day before, as if every day is new, and each one behind, never happened. In a dream, I am swimming in the ocean—I am not sure where Dallas is, but he is close. There are military helicopters that are painted in camouflage green that first fly above, then they circle around; then they become submarines, vibrating the water I cannot escape. Psychic Powers: The next morning, from T.V., I learn there are dolphins trapped in some river in New Jersey. The state, if needed, decides they may herd the animals back to the ocean with sonar from boats circling around and with choppers, startling them from above.

DIFFERENCE

When the gum on the white tile has turned black, splotches flat and hard as rock, the world is a panorama of porn. The video booth doors open to cars, some to grease on the face, long flat hair, shaved heads, clits and tongues, and of course thick cocks that fill screen after screen. In a void: everything is working except what needs to be worked on. What needs to be assembled are the pieces of the plate that broke over the head of a boy in Florida who is forced to participate in the gang rape of his mother. Black, twelve, a pre-teen, 10, 15, at-large, 2 caught, then 3, a 4th by DNA from a spent condom. A black mother and her son walk a mile, until a hospital, two hours after the attack. The boys poured cleaning supply in his eyes: Was it bleach, Pine Sol? I find *ammonia* and *soap* stuffed in her. They were going to burn them, but they couldn't find a lighter. The sun has not come out for a day, and driving in rain with G.P.S. is easy, because the rain does not matter as much as the blue display which reveals how big and complicated it is becoming to sort between the questions: What were the shooters trying to erase? What were the rapists trying to rape? The speaker in the project tries to say something. Maybe that is the point, the body never really having a chance at being human, rendered, read, filled and filled, and we fill and fill, and those boys how many, twelve, fourteen, "They hit him and made him do stuff," the woman's brother said, "and when he didn't do it, they made his mom do stuff."[4] The couches are big and thick, some brown, red, some leather. In this room, there are men who look lost, who are as lost as trying to arrange this loss, as lost as the one at the door, who won't let his pants fall. Or another who says, You missed it, when he came in a small, silent fountain that pierced the porno-light. Covered by a soft body: What the speaker wants to say: *Move*, but says, *Daddy*—Facsimile—The mother is an immigrant. She was not from there. She went to church. Her son was good, the neighbors said.

4. Dwayne Robinson. "Victims' Family Reveals Some Gruesome Details of Attack" *Palm Beach Post*. 8 July 2007.

I've decided to try not to stop. Completing the drive south, on Route 91, from Northampton to South Hadley, my body clean, Bikram-sweat out, or my valves flushed after therapy, there's a twinned emptiness in my sense of having left it all on the mat or in the mini-Zen garden on my analyst's end table. At the scenic view stop, the cops who cruise in rarely exit their cars, or if they do, and you're sitting alone inside of one, at times, they tap on the window and ask, "Is everything OK?" And it's always okay. I never move quickly, and sometimes circumvent such tapping by reorganizing my tennis rackets or my toiletries case, or whatever's in the back. I never let my heart run fast enough to move me into awkward angles and fissures enough to get caught.

Scenic route for sex = Big White Men in Semis = Or more simply, old, married men with rings that catch the sun in the forest—these men, though, call it the woods. "Wanna take a walk in the woods?" I'm not certain if I found this place on my own, or on Squirt.org, but I do know that as soon as I first drove past it, and saw the lines of cars, the trucks hunched next to the guard rail, I knew I would pull in and park.

Lauren Berlant and Michael Warner write that " . . . the queer world is a space of entrances, exits, unsystemized lines of acquaintances, projected horizons, typifying examples, alternate routes, blockages, incommensurate geographies."[5] In a sense, what I want to do here is to capture my body's own particular relationship to many such spaces. But let me qualify what I mean. In doing this, I am mapping out the space of decision and indecision in my own body, its pull, its urge, oscillating until I decide or feel, to stop before entering such an exchange, route, alternate, a stage of the cruise, of cruising that marks the split, the

5. Lauren Berlant and Michael Warner. "Sex in Public," *Critical Inquiry* Vol. 24, No. 2 (Winter, 1998) 558.

proverbial fork in my road: Do I go to Panera, home, keep forward after the red light, hope it's green so I don't have to think, or not make the turn into what is pulling me onto, then off of the highway?

While driving, I am thinking about the distance that I cover, some five miles or so from the exit to the scenic route's stop, the fast stretch of road where cars speed from one exit to another, all collecting at the bottleneck, its tight grip that slows the traffic to expose the long view of the boats in the boat dock, and behind these boats, more green, more field.

This vista, a layering of trees cascading to the highway's floor, reminds me that I, here, have time to wonder, that my body can saturate, stew in the promise of who might be waiting at the top of the mountain, or in his car, where I place this urge, an urge that says I am retreating into what I need, like Adrian Piper's *Mythic Being*, who thinks in a white thought bubble, "It is only because of the defects in my personality that I can finally say this to you. I am protected and strengthened by my inadequacy. I am secure, smugly secure, for my personal flaws will constitute a more than adequate defense against whatever your response might be to what I have to say to you." I am willing to give up, what seems at the moment, like everything, or escape from anything, marking papers, writing, any kind of work, to get closer to some fantasy about my body in space: as resembling the idea of your wife, the one at home, she in the Capris, as happy and plump as you are wide and grey.

Daddy, this is about the body's language in languish, or languish in driving what I can't control but what I remap by resisting. *Resist/resist/resist/resist/resist/resist*—it's what Sonia Sanchez, touched by some inalienable grief gone deep, bluebird out of a window, eyes gone back depressed in a head—is she saying, leave it all alone? Or is it through the litany, throat, hum that she charts the tension not in resisting, as in letting it go, but in the act of letting it hover?

Being near the forest, or being in the woods' proximity, to what it promises (desire, touch, release, view, escape, bush, thorn, tic, dirt) exposes my body across one field into another. The map enlarges: I recall when I lived in and first moved to Manhattan, walking from Penn Station down to the Village or up from Penn Station to Port Authority, and winding up to any of the bathrooms, which were rarely tearooms as late as

1996 with any real portent, nothing often close to action, homeless sweet decay, plastic fixtures, walls, long melted away into the peripatetic 42nd street now gone to the Disneyfication Chip Delany captures in *Times Square Red, Times Square Blue*. He laments in the fall of zones of sexual and social possibility, particularly, in such realms as the porn movie house, "a 'social excess' . . . beneficial to some small part of it (a margin outside the margin)," an argument he continues, "that allows them to be dismissed—and physically smashed and flattened: They are relevant only to that margin. No one else cares" (90).

As I oscillated in the smash and flat, I recalled the pain in my heel spurs building in my Bostonians, a fat daddy with a pungent foreskin, who offered to my then soon visiting parents that they could stay in a hotel he managed in New Jersey, for sixty dollars a night after we were done in his car in the parking garage. Or, exiting the 4 or 5 at the Fulton stop, and not going home to Brooklyn, but to walk down to Maiden Lane, the small set of steps, then the teeny elevator that creaked up to the Wall Street Sauna, and how in that elevator, I felt I was traveling in a cardboard box, creeping up to the men, squat, round, heavy, white, fraying towels. Even before I got there, this promise would tug, such from a refraction of glasses or stubble on any stop on any train, anywhere, taking me out of my doctoral studies bee line, or back midtown to the 4 or 5 to the Grand Hyatt Marriott, pretending to talk on the pay phones, or actually calling a voice mail box on the very same phones, looking to find any silver daddy to eat out my ass in the middle of his otherwise busy afternoon.

There are two discernible sets of trails that arc up the side of the mountain, the ground cleaved by human footpaths in the dirt, or snow in winter, the crunch of the ice below my Hugo Boss boots, the black strap that winds through the leather, and the heavy motorcycle tread keeping me from slipping. One trail leads to another, up the hill, where on top there is a telephone pole, wires, dry grass that leads out into the backside of Mount Tom, to a place I have only driven, an abandoned amusement park that is now concrete and peeking out, rebar.

By day, I look out at the large water cylinder in the distance to see if I can see my home. I wait for trucks, cars with equipment on the back, ladders. But I've stopped here at night, and I can't make out any faces. The town has blocked one entrance of the mountain with timber, logs and brush piled up, like steel wool stuffed in a wall to keep out the flow of mouse or rat. The cop is in stealth mode. He rolls by slowly, and shines the light on me, and the biker in bulky leather. I'm outside, we're talking, and I lean into the blinding light, and neither of us scurry or turn. His name is George, but he says *Gheyahhge*, and he does not answer the telephone on Thursday nights when he becomes Tracy, fishnets and short skirts on Fridays. He says I can go online to a site I don't remember, *to See Me Tracy*, but all I want is to know whether or not he is cut. He tells me, yes, and about his little, shaved patch. The sky is black and clear, the night, humid.

"Give me 15 seconds." This is what the thin, white woman breathes out from the seat in front of me in the *Art Cinema*. She's riding an older man, grey, tall, a single white stripe down each leg of his black sweats. Her hair, in the screen's light, is wavy, grey too, but tied down to her head. Other men move into the space surrounding them, a zone we edge into from our seats, and even though I want him, I listen to her breath as her sweater and jacket drop to her waist. She pulls her shirt over her head, and off. How do I write the distance between my body, sealed in my "Paper" denim jeans, and my white Adidas, black striped on white nylon tight weave, with a red tongue, the small black logo laid in the heel? How do I modulate an occasion, here, about power, its recognition of her vulnerability, or pleasure, and the questions that rotate in the dark: *who wants her, and who, him?*

Is my desire caught in the pleasure (or at least the sound) of her riding him? Or does it hover in her moans, or press in the many hands that move in to touch her? I notice she's not looking at the film, but neither am I. She's looking around, and I'm looking at her lover. I don't want to join them. I want to be her. No one touches her unless she wants to be touched. She kisses her man deeply before, I think, she takes off to the bathroom.

Recently, I've become obsessed with watching amateur porn clips on my laptop. I find them on a myriad of sites to include "Slutload," "xHamster," "Tube8," and "Sextube," each of which features a variety of miniature screens that promise, in detail, whatever the viewer desires. Once, after not finding what I needed by typing "older," or "old man," or "grandpa sex"—I tried "amateur gangbang"—I typed in "theater." I found "Dawn," an older red-headed amateur star who features in her own series of videos, made while (she says) her husband films her getting fucked by anonymous men in theaters. Dawn likes the older, bigger ones, like I do.

In one thumbnail "Theatre Cream Pie," cum eventually suspends from her puffed-cunt like the ooze out of a jelly-filled doughnut, and she's very chubby, and the men, they are all fat, too, stout guts, sweatshirts, some in camouflage, some in shorts, some in whatever ship grey and dusty blue windbreaker they fit—some in belts, some in whatever jeans, or Dockers, some small cocks, some bigger, uncut, pubes clipped, some natural, all hungry for Dawn on her back who is ready for it all.

In the graininess of each scene, I want to be Dawn, too, her soft, open body, wet and revealed by flashlight, pumped by daddy and trucker, security and random Tom alike. Though she is being *used*, I think, she, too, is a *user*. She gets up, lays some mustached long-haired grey dad down on a table, where she just got trained, and sucks him off. Gobs of his spunk geyser out. She spits out what she caught. Dawn turns to the camera, not really looking into it, lost in the middle of her and her husband's fantasies come true.

In the cinema, I think about space, the various ways that bodies interact with one another, and the modes through which they intersect. How do I mark my own being through the matrix of what at any moment depends on what the couple in the theater performs? How do I mark the space between my body and theirs, my legs crossed and hidden, my eyes wandering around, my body in the frenzy, wondering how close I can get to her riding without his hand waving me away?

A large, mid 50's cross-dresser sits in the back, eating from a bag of chips, loud enough for me to hear his crunching over the moans of the movie. The boldest among us, he comes over in his tent dress and tiny clutch to sit right next to them. I reach out to touch one of the men straddled above the couple, who've moved, now, a few rows back. Fat, bald, big belly, beard, this new visitor's pants are open, his little un-hard cock out into the air.

Online, I click in search of old men like him, simple, un-pierced, thick, or old men who fuck men, and then I note the links, try to ignore the massive dick pushing into the pulsing "Fleshlight" ad. I find myself viewing "destroyed pussies," "creampie," "anal ownage," peering into the repeating blonde, gaping, her availability, my point of immersion, to be Dawn, or the thin, white woman, riding, to take in what they have, to absorb what they make me feel in the clutch of desire.

A busload of people is about to smash into a cement wall upon which is playing a movie, such an unlikely, impossible impromptu drive-in, featured in the middle of a highway. I am watching this unfold, attempting to see how every part of this dream is pieced together before the moment of impact. This moment is difficult to trace, and it becomes even more so, to think about this as tracking a poetics in which every piece of the dream is fragile, and the narrative, although promising insight into process and statement, shifts from the point of origin to openings beyond any inevitable collision.

Call it form, or a first form, or a sense, or perhaps, even, a sensibility: In the dream, a man is caught in a crime. From on the bus, I look down at the cap of this man, whose head is slightly gray and puffy underneath the bill that I will eventually lift to make sure he's black. I first see him about twenty yards in front of me a few moments before I notice some commotion up ahead, and realize as I move closer that the trouble is he has smashed an old, white lady in her face. *How could you do this? Didn't you know?* Intractable trope, submerged in my mind—how did I get from moving by bus to foot? How will I later, or earlier, depending on the pace of my dream, figure out a way to direct myself through this readily accessible crime unearthed in my unconscious?

On the bus, a group of white men warn the younger ones that there will be a crash—and one says to the others—perhaps including me in the warning—that you have to look behind you to see what will happen. *Sing a warning*, one of them says. The distance between song and the wall extends through the message and the song's meaning, or at least its intention as a warning about how and where I function in dream space. I realize this is not a mix-up, and I am as fearful of what's to come as I am of who I am.

What kind of poet are you? How do you say, I am a Black poet? How do you say that being a Black poet is how I am also an Asian and Gay poet? How do you say, I am not interested in anything but the sky at one moment, and the complications of intentionally wanting to soil a bathroom wall, or to hack up on someone's face, in the next? How do you say, I have given over to the labor of the exhausted black body in one form of writing after another? How do you say, I have splinters to pull from my brain, as I attempt to occupy and evade? How do you say, I am lost in the complications of my birth, that for me, being a poet is tied to the experience of, at this moment, purposefully moving in what Myung Mi Kim, in *Commons*, names as the "circulatory spaces," somewhere in the "storehouse of the human," what I see as the complicated archive of experience that is freeing, yet held in relief to what binds me to root and wire. How do you say, there is no safety net, and the more clearly you delineate, the more it becomes harder to make an honest living in the world where you have to eat, pay bills, and love?

Communities can sometimes serve as illusions. For instance, writing into a wall of meaning, writing oneself into a listserv or even a Facebook page, or onto a group of people in some space however imagined, assumes that you really care about being a part of the community, when in the end, it's not about communicating, but being, and most of the time, one exists alone, at least in the work of writing. I think if I had my choice, I'd want to forever be in an "art cloud" as my friend, the artist, T.D. once confessed being inside of. It is then that I smell D. come out of the shower and feel the smell of soap and sleep washed away and realize I am not anywhere near my family, and being on the job market prevents me from seeing them for many months as I am split between homes, coasts, desks. Are you settled enough to create with such distractions? Out of the cloud, into my bed.

I feel this raging internal chaos, and I can't quite identify the source, only that my dream life is on the move in multiple registers, while I try to rest. I cannot contain, nor do I understand what it means, or just how the fields shift. Out of inadequacy, out of fear, pondering laziness, I sit at a table being questioned in the dream by another poet. T.M. asks, *what's your origin?* I do not answer this question, and a few questions later, I say *no comment*, and I can't quite say what I want to say in the dream. Something haunts me as I awake, but it is not the interrogation, it's what happens in the dream, in the space of an impossible conversation that takes shape, one wall after another built by way of saying something like, *my poetics emerges from this.*

There are rows of tables that hold sound mixers, and projectors that shoot onto screens. On one screen, I am moving, dancing, when my work is being read aloud. An interview gives my bio, somewhere saying, I teach at L. And I do not. What you must claim is your place even though that place is porous, and often not of your own choosing. I know that what I am arguing for is as hard to identify as the pressure point of morning gasses, sleep in the eyes, a stiff and hurting back, but what I do realize is that, in the end, I have to wake.

"You Suck," is what I say as I walk across a warehouse space to see D.L. in the dream. She is busy in a corner working on her own material, watching a screen, looking up at it, focusing on her internal self, mining the self's projected composition. Her actions are a reminder to me to keep doing me. *Do You*—she seems to say. J.K. is in the dream, and he's urging me on, too. And since he's chosen the opaque, the oblique as a primary mode in his writing, I listen.

Motion, I realize, is a killer. But I move from one place to the next, try to rest, and then move some more. I keep a space for my poems clear. I exhaust, vacate. I finish up with one thing so that I may move onto another, one burden layered on top of the next, one weight on top of the same, my body on top of the threat of hitting a wall in a dream. In another, I ride on a boat, speeding across a brown lake, pulling up mud by hand as we cruise through the water. I try to explain to the passengers that the earth below the water is rich and clear—and I exemplify by pulling out of the deep, a scoop of mud, some of it floating like oil on the surface—*You can use it on your skin*, I tell the passengers as I smear some on my face.

In the dream, a game is also being played—it's a pre-emptive game. Rows of teens are on another bus, and in fact, in a caravan of buses, all singing some strange version of "Mary Had a Little Lamb," as a round, and I look at the lyrics appearing on my cell phone screen, and I see these complicated quatrains that bundle up on one another. The bus divides into a caravan of cars.

I will watch them smash into the wall now in front of me, every inch of the disaster I forecast, all of it unfolding as I look at them about to hit.

The old black man in the dream is cold. I don't really identify with this version of the self. I ask him what he wears, and he says that he wears "L," and because I wear "M," I cannot give him my shirt to keep warm. But he has done so much for us.

A row of us seated at the table are trying to eat our pastry and croissant in peace at the café where we belong, and no one can help him, though I want to, but he has grown too large and cold for my shirt. I will walk away with this feeling of not being able to cover him, my cold body, his, turned away, how I will never stop seeing, nor warning, nor tracking the dream between movement, collision, and life.

Axing the seed's shell, I lay into the dream-object with what feels like the weight of an anvil. Cracking it, splitting when I wake from the threshold of sleep, I turn to Robert Hass's book, *Praise*, to encounter "Heroic Simile," and drift into these lines: "When the swordsman fell in Kurosawa's *Seven Samurai*/in the gray rain/in Cinemascope and Tokugawa dynasty,/ he fell straight as a pine, he fell/ . . . " (1-3). To rise from a parallel free fall from sleep, my dreamed axe shattering the smallest of things, my lolling into the Samurai's drop, is perhaps why, before I left home, I packed Proust. In mapping my relationship with sleep's dimensions, one route is clear in *Swann's Way*, when the author seeks, "to savour, in a momentary glimmer of consciousness, the sleep which lay heavy upon the furniture, the room, the whole of which I formed . . . " (5).

In this world—the extenuation of consciousness/unconsciousness through objects, the space between *dream* and *awake*—is a poetics of slowing down perception enough to hold the shrill of crows that *caw caw caw caw* outside my window, or the voices that fade from a party dying down the distant hall of a house in which I chose to retreat. Perhaps I am after what Laura Riding followed into "the journey to truth—to the plane of utterance on which human speaking spoke the language of being with a full, universal explicitness of sense"(*Collected Poems*, 5).

In *Daddy Attacks*, a hairy chested daddy breathes *Sí, Sí, Sí, Sí,* as his lips curl and he drives in to make his young lover cum. I stop my run on the black cement trail, to watch the arc of a bald eagle's head dip over her nest. After she tucks back in, I clap my hands to startle the bird to look back out. In a draft of a poem, called, "Drawing," I write about filling in a center again and again black, each striation of the pen clarifying, as though I am drawing what I want to say in layers of ink that settle into a dark corner of a sketched face. Filling in this vision opens another, the memory of an old man in the shower at the Y, his flaccid uncut dick, thick, and his balls hanging down big as a bull's. He stepped on his trunks on the shower floor. Rinsed, when he bent over to pick them up, his thigh skin in between, shown brown, from years of movement, peddling, walking, shifting.

> *Sometimes the poetic process is like drawing,*
>   *marking over and over, filling,*
>   *to make the subject break from its linearity,*
>   *like writing into the center of a centrifuge,*
>   *until what I want to appear is what's left.*

I want to trace a set of aesthetic instances where my body touches language, where desire delineates in form, from sleepy stupor to drawn subject. What enacts when I let go is what releases when my body reacts, giving up as I linger in the screen, nest, down the hall, or on the gym shower floor, my senses open to the poem that comes.

The chubby son in front of me, cow-licked & hotel sleepy, asks his tall, muscled father, "Is it possible to start a fire with just your hands?" Not pondering in front of his row of French toast, he says to the boy, "No." To my right, a flip-flopped teenage girl is the big daughter of a giant in flesh tone pressure socks. He's thankful to have brought an extra pair of shorts after spilling syrup all down his front. He moans, "Son of a gun," before wiping himself down with a busser's towel. The daughter says, "I'm sorry," twice, in the sweetest voice, before she adds, "The syrup's more watery today." On my left, in white New Balance sneakers, a fat and bald husband fills to stretch his marble bordered *Florida* Beefy-T. In my periphery are four buckets of Philly Cream Cheese, four sausages swimming in the mix of syrup and a pastry basking beside more French toast. The husband crumb-lipped, puffs, "I need some water." "They'll come, you have to ask," the wife says, sucks a pineapple cube and tells her man, "This is good." "It looks sweet," he returns. For me, poetry is in these found places of being, discovered by taking notes, sometimes of the everyday drama in how a people consume, taking in what they want in some morning, while I do, too, in the clink of talk, fork and plate. I keep thinking of fire, the image of hands rubbing together, the sound of fingerprint skin on palms, the feel of fat, blood, and bone within. I find myself in the center of looking into shapes that surround me. I attempt to make patterns, layering one into the next, often with such questions: How to participate, to point, to pull back, to listen? Where do I fit in between these tables: eater, poet, judge, hungry person, floater? I want to tell the son, *Yes!* I return to the buffet—even after my omelet, two pieces of French toast, two strips of bacon, a bowl of fruit, a *Refresh* tea—to get more. My last plate is nothing but a few Honeydew melon chunks, two spoons of corned beef hash & a mini-muffin. As the couple is about to leave, I pull my laptop close into my body. The wife struggles to get up—the husband, standing, holds her hands and pulls, wedging her out. Walking, her body is bent to the left, partly collapsed, turning, exiting in the same direction.

POETICS AFTER THIS QUESTION: HOW DO WE INVENT THE LANGUAGE OF RACIAL IDENTITY—THAT IS, NOT NECESSARILY CONSTRUCTING THE "SCENE OF INSTRUCTION" ABOUT RACE, BUT CREATE THE LINGUISTIC MATERIAL OF RACIAL SPEECH/THOUGHT?

for Claudia Rankine

The story is a familiar one. You have even found it to be repeated so often that it has become ingrained in your psyche as fact, the same old, same old, the usual, you think. Sometimes it begins with a joke over the phone, *Were you in Arizona?* Or a question, *What did they say you were doing?* Or it ends in an apartment you made it back to in the middle of the night: *I'm glad you're safe.* There are attempts to comfort you even more, because your friends see that, despite your escape, you're still shaking: *Do you want me to make you some tea?*

But if you are on the other side of this story, you might be saying to yourself, *not again, I did nothing wrong.* In fact, you have done everything right, so right, that when you confront what you cannot control, you must learn to relax, breathe with enough care and measure so that your body conceals its shaking—but your eyes, those are another matter. You think, *Please don't dilate*—at least not wide enough to draw any more attention to your very existence—in the wrong place at the wrong time. Of course, what's connected to the depth of this realization is that you are never where you completely belong, but you must learn to modify, to make do, to make clear your plot and push, what you read and write, map how you travel, go, go, and go. Above all, you have learned to not become crushed by having to make these adjustments in the face of a constant, sometimes blatant, sometimes quiet duress, and to remain as elegant and articulate as you are in tact. Perhaps in the end, that's all that you want after the performance, after the teaching, after the ride, after the dinner, after the wine, after the dessert, after the nap, after the errand.

The night is cool, but from all the work of remaining stable, you are very, very dizzy. This dizziness is not from the wine—you drank reasonably, a bottle of a light, white, split with two of your closest friends, the shared hummus and Armenian Snapper, the perfect olives and Baklava. It was, after all, for your birthday, and the evening's indulgence was not what led you into the dizziness. There are other facts that have nothing to do with the dinner that edges you into the realm of being spectacle, a history of spectacle over which you have no control, things that your face, body, grooming and circumstance cannot, at this moment, elide.

You are a visitor—the afternoon sun in Los Angeles is bright and you find yourself settling into the view of one stunning mountain range after another. At night, you are still driving the big, white rental car, trying to figure out how to maneuver the wide turns at this 2 AM hour, but you cannot find your way back to your friend's apartment. A pressure builds, perhaps the pressure of the self about to enjoy the late night, double dessert. You want to keep celebrating. Who knows when you will see your friends again? But you have to get back to square the bill. You have to pack. You get caught up in the struggle of trying to fill the gas tank up to match the 3/4th's notch on the car's check sheet. Out to gather donuts, two chocolate glazed, a croissant, one old fashioned (bought a glazed cruller by mistake), one glazed bowtie, and since the woman who looks like your mother tells you the cinnamon raisin rolls are fresh and warm, you get that for yourself.

The tank's gauge never indicates the right amount, and the sky above Glendale doesn't look threatening, then you feel the approach of the slowing car of which you are also so familiar, a familiarity you anticipate by feeling the tightening around your heart. You sigh, not out of relief, but to stay calm. You slow down your step, and then a light bursts—*Can I talk to you a minute? We've had some complaints about your driving.* I got lost. I had to fill the rental car. I'm tired, a little sleepy. *That's not good.* I'm Ronaldo Wilson, and I'm traveling. I got turned around. I'm sorry. *Are you on probation?* No, I'm a professor. I gave a talk today, and taught a class. We just gave a big performance, and soon, we have to leave and catch a red-eye home. I live in New York.

Cathy Caruth points out that, "Traumatic memories are the unassimilated scraps of overwhelming experiences, which need to be integrated with existing mental schemes, and be transformed into narrative language. It appears that, in order for this to occur successfully, the traumatized person has to return to the memory often in order to complete it."[6] *Did I get away*, you think? The event, you correctly suspect will occur again, and though will leave you, you continue to hope, untouched by hand, baton, bullet or fist, what cycles is your narrative's constant repetition and spread. Your sister says she feels sad, and says something like, *You can't forget, you're a black man.* This makes you sad, which comes from, you think, the source of her sadness. Pulled over in the middle of the day, stopped on the side of the road in Elk Grove. *You didn't do anything wrong. It's your car. You're not a bad person.* But you think this is not your story, because you understand how to talk to them. Contrite, you're wearing a black compression sweat suit, and you have finished yoga, and the last time you were pulled over, in South Hadley, you were marked, in the officers, box "B" for Black, and the time before that, in Northampton, you were marked "W" for White, and in each case, you were able to say how sorry you were for this or that, and in court, you beat the ticket by saying, *I want to apologize for taking up the court's time, and I'm not here to challenge the officer, or to deny that I drove through the turning lane. I hope you'll consider my perfect driving record, and that I simply made a mistake—if the court could just grant me leniency, this one time, I would be so very grateful.*

Sorry Boss, Yassuh, I didn't mean nothin' by it, you learn to say in the most protracted ways. Once, as a teen, you are in an old Nova, and actually think, after getting pulled over, what if I sound like a Valley girl? In Sacramento, *I'm borrowing my dad's car, and I'm really late, I'm so, so sorry*, or, once, more recently, you are profiled in Elk Grove, in a BMW Z4, and once you are cruising in a train station in New York, carrying a red duffle bag: *Do you mind telling me where you're going?*

I have done no wrong, at least not a wrong I am aware of, or I got turned around a couple of times. I pulled over to let another car pass. I am coming from a class, or simply walking down a street. There is no violence—no one gets hurt. There is always violence, and someone always gets killed. The earthquake is inevitable. The toll grows. No elbow jabs, but there is the possibility of an elbow jab. No big black bears tazed in the night, no license is asked for. There is no report. They will not touch you, but sometimes they

6. Cathy Caruth, *Trauma: Explorations in Memory* (Baltimore: The Johns Hopkins University Press, 1995) 153.

do touch you. One shakes your hand, while another refuses, crossing his arms when you reach out to try to shake his. Where will the pieces of this narrative coalesce?

You do not belong. Go away, run. For the listener, there are related narratives that capture the formation of the self, constructed in the moment of being pulled over, its many remnants, its cycling reminders, its relentless endurance. Caruth discusses the work of Pierre Janet, pointing out that, "He proposed that traumatic recall remains insistent and unchanged to the precise extent that it has never, from the beginning, been fully integrated into understanding."[7] So that here, the scene of instruction in accounting for this old narrative, or the many that surround it, bleeds into what it means to be forever marked by the fact of one's very existence. Building around this existence is a scene of constant interpolation, slipping in, where one slips away, examining how one escapes and begins to process the story of survival, from contrition to understanding—to engage and disengage with this story, the same old, same old, that which will always be familiar, and that which will continue to remain.

7. Ibid.

There are versions of a self, here, which I'd like to expose, a self that says, I'm attached to a history of undeniable oppression, a force so systematic and relentless that I've had to master an ability to speak from inside this force without cause to display any direct reflex or alarm. In my search for what and who I hate, or why I'd like to speak into this hatred is that I find used terms, and rote stances, like the experience is "tragicomic," or note how one is bolted to the blues, and that another never seems afraid of being read as calm in the whirling winds of it all, because one is rarely engaged as a cool survivor, but still barely on edge, which in most cases, is quite different from being the winner, a chair, or a recipient.

I once took a bus to Patterson, New Jersey for a poetry symposium. It's quite famous. One poet who's edited many anthologies which feature underrepresented folk, many women, many of color, some queer, and all from the same yet wide and varied diaspora was on a panel about the production of such anthologies. She said she was tired of the same questions again and again, and I loved her answer by way of her own dogged query: "Who's in? Who's out? Who Cares?"

My oppression, one says, I must make beautiful.

Oh void.

Avoid.

This here, *"This here, niggah"*—is a version of a self that attempts to translate pathos, but is often caught up in the bog of what gets so quickly equipped for market, performed in the line of such predictable narratives meant to soothe—One is like:

I am a boy that was beaten to a pulp, and/or I pray or prayed just after this beating, or I can't wait to sing in tune with the many songs I come from, many that you will recognize, songs to entertain you, a song that will punctuate my formation into or as the material of what's not left behind, but banked for easy retrieval.

     Piece of Shit.

Pile.
   Bile.
      Vile.

In my Doctoral Orals exam, I successfully defended three bibliographical lists: (1) 20th Century and Contemporary African American Poetry; (2) The Black Body in Contemporary African American Visual Culture; and (3) Autobiography: Myth, Memoir, Manifesto. Some of the details are important. First, that I was the first in my PhD program to use visual art and other images in the Orals defense. Of the wide glossy photocopies with which I covered the seminar table, these stand out: Serena Williams, blonde then, and sinewy-young, pounding a backhand so that her muscles rip, perfectly through the shot. Another, the artist Adrian Piper, in her "Mythic Being" series, thin, donning a perfectly blown Afro, faux mustache and aviator shades, flipping, via triptych, a similarly thin white man to the ground.

Second, I described how a number of critical arguments about race and abstraction, loss and defilement (in both poetry and prose) informed these photographs, or at least my beginnings of an argument about them, how I was starting to imagine writing a poetics of the black body as a field of reiterative violation—in other words, or as was my hope, to reveal how Williams's and Piper's work and play would serve as interlocutors into my project, where their performances (in various kinds of repetitions) served as a way to think closely about form and intent.

After a successful defense, in which I received kisses, hugs, and "highest distinction," I was later under the natural light in the atrium at the Pierpont Morgan Library, where my dissertation advisor treated me to a congratulatory light lunch, of I think it was grilled trout and a dark vegetable, or maybe they were roots on a plate, white wine, my knife falling through the perfect finish.

And I would ride on a cloud through the day to the end of the semester party, down to the "Revels," in the campus auditorium, where two of my friends, well ahead of that night, volunteered to D.J. the event. One was in the program. One wasn't. They brought CD's and playlists. I don't recall the exact details of what happened despite some annoying requests for them to change up the set. Maybe it was about them keeping the music hip hop and house against some bigger wishes, or I was feeling super aggressive, or too happy, or dancing too hard, when one of my fellow PhD students thought I was hired as part of what he imagined to be a rented D.J. crew! None of us he figured were graduate students—too rich, too urbane, or maybe simply, I-the-help, or I was the Jiggin' Hype Man not taking his requests for whatever-the-fuck seriously. Maybe I told him to wait, that he couldn't have everything he wanted. Maybe I said nothing, my body as code, my refusal, my reveling in achieving "highest distinction," and still celebrating in the university's lower auditorium, as I was earlier in the restaurant's atrium, chilling with my advisor a few hours before.

"You Piece of Shit!" After he called me this, I don't recall how close I was to his face, or if I would really hit him, or if I told him then I was a student, too, but I did say that language between us had failed, that physical violence was the only appropriate answer to what he said to me, so I asked him, quite plainly, shaking, puffed like a baboon, "Should I hit you in your jaw?"

"No." Primate backed down.

Back in Black Mountain, a child will
smack your face

Back in Black Mountain, a child will
smack your face

Babies Cryin' for liquor, and all the birds
sing bass.[8]

Though I think if I perform this enduring ballad of my intrinsic sadness, you will buy it, and celebrate my anger, especially if I recount other instances of my need in having to live like this along the way, a life, in the end, that makes me nice, makes me like you, or smile, things that are mostly real. Some quick facts that you must already realize: I listen to all types of music. I drive a modest car, or I have a father from whom I am most certainly estranged, and, or in my lack of silence as a mode of discovery, I project my regret and subservience in a worn form that is recognizable from start to finish. I'm continuous. Stanzaic. I couplet. I title. Each. I'm full of it.

I will not kill you. Love leads me. I will not murder, when you least expect it. You will not be face raped, nor will you feel ashamed for looking so closely at my file, my growing absent hair, my chest, shaved. Look into my eyes.

I work hard. I'm an open book. I want to teach at your institution, even though you say to me over breakfast in the hotel lobby down the street from the massive windowed suite where you put me up, "It's all about luck," and when you call, and I miss you because I'm teaching, and you say call back, and you leave me your office and your cell, and you do call me back, and it's not too long a wait, just enough time for me to imagine seriously carrying your 3/3 load on my back, but when you catch me, where I wait, like a frayed baby bird, starved in a packed nest, you don't say, "Ronaldo, we can offer you the position, or Ronaldo,

8. Smith, Bessie. "Black Mountain Blues" (J.C. Johnson), 1930.

we've offered it to someone else," like you said you'd say. Instead, you tell me, "We've decided to run the search again next year, and we really want you to apply again."

In Ralph Ellison's *Invisible Man*, this moment comes to mind. It's when the protagonist wakes up in the hospital somewhere near the Liberty Paint factory after the boiler blows, and after wrestling with the crazy old super—a knife scene, a whole nightmare, where he's attacked by that psycho-black who rules the basement. After the dentures chatter on the floor, and the blade slides out of the scene, he arises under this stark light, which, for me, does not illuminate. It's not what instructs, it's what bleeds from the event, the shadow language of realization between what's obvious—fact—and what comes into view, recalled, as one drifts from one realm of consciousness into another. A name. A body. A location. An experiment. A self on the run away and towards another self, becoming a self in an optic white box. A rabbit. To wake up and to realize the saliency of the fictive, as in the line from Cornelius Eady's poem "Brutal Imagination," *I float in forces / I can't always control.*

Funding, Shmunding, and I think liar, liar pants on fire, though I WIKI see you did select, and yet, another of the same, of someone who looks like another version of one of you, younger, but as white, or maybe a little tougher version of the same, the voice still safe, the credentials, or the calls don't matter. He'll visit. Like you, he'll wear a big black beard. I won't ever work there. A friend of mine will. We will remain smooth, float in and out, though you do get one of us.

On YouTube, I find the playful scene in which this clever beaver face chomps and reads in a fast food joint. How to be myself to the last degree, when the space for the coy and the humorous is always wound around the long joke of some circumstance out of my own construction and desire. An intense sadness or maybe it is nervousness that fills me, but still I shower, and still I float towards the mass dinner, like the one blurred in the pamphlets, to be shot at the table, to be insulted in the kitchen, swept by the wind on the trail, the crack of the tree branch triggering me to run away from the sound.

When they say, "It has to be the right fit," it does matter. When they say, you are too loud, and how did you get that, or how did you get here, and will you stay? And there are echoes, drawers shutting through the night, sounds that travel inside the place where you can't bear to know I exist, noises that cannot be muffled or silenced, shifts, creaks that mark my being, scratches behind the door you try to block by woolen blanket.

When they say you can't go into the pool, because you are not us, the WHITES ONLY sign also burns into your eyes, even though you've never seen one, for real, up close, in your time, so you learn to make alternative moves, evade history, improvise, start over, run, do wind sprints—no matter what, get the run in, refuse to soundproof your side of the adjoining room. Or yoga. Move around whatever you imagine. Return to language. Return to song, even on the run that winds you around a park in a suburb full of the same of those who never look or sound like you, and at the end, you stretch away in the grass, on a hill, in the earliest light.

> *Don't worry about a thing,*
> *'Cause every little thing gonna be all right.*
> *Singin': "Don't worry about a thing,*
> *'Cause every little thing gonna be all right!*[9]

"All socio-ideological analyses agree on the deceptive nature of literature (which deprives them of a certain pertinence): the work is finally always written by a socially disappointed or powerless group, beyond the battle because of its historical, economic, political situation: literature is the expression of this disappointment." So says Barthes[10]; and Bernstein, in *A Poetics*, who describes two distinct camps of poets, those who refine tradition, and those who remain dissatisfied.[11]

I don't say this to you when you call, but maybe you know how you made me feel, that I was proud to be a finalist, one of three, yet again. Forget serendipity. As much as luck, maybe I want you to feel safe, and when you hear me sing, you should lie back and feel in every case soothed. Imagine hard, me reading so many

9. Bob Marley and the Wailers. "Three Little Birds," *Exodus*, 1977.
10. Barthes, Roland. *Pleasure of the Text*. (New York: Hill & Wang, 1975).
11. Bernstein, Charles. *A Poetics*. (Cambridge: Harvard University Press, 1992).

books and internalizing so many ideas, and trudging so long a road just to slip in by the skin off my back—or as I'm reminded *by my teeth*—to your front door.

My grandmother said when she was traveling with her family somewhere in the South, and she stopped to get coffee, they said, "Sure, we'll give you some," and they got a cup to give her, a cup laced thick with spider webs. And she said she went around back, and rinsed the cup out by hose, and dried it, and returned to the front counter of the diner to get her coffee. And I hated it, and you, when I arrived on some rainy night to your city, to your campus suite, to discover no soap anywhere inside, and I hated walking through the rain, to buy my own soap from the 7-11, a borrowed umbrella from the black guards at the front desk, and only a few hours later, I would need to be clean and clear to give you all I had that morning in my talk and the Q&A, to be so smart and socially sound through the rest of the day and into the night of dinner, so pleasant, so smiley. And the next day, I would do it all again.

On the other side, one self blogs about a success, "I did not get the fellowships I wanted, but I got a job," and then prattles along, describing the campus visit, cheerily feeling, so stupidly, as if it were like being on a cycle of dates, falling in "love," again and again with each on the hiring committee—finally, that satisfied self resounds, "MISSION ACCOMPLISHED!" I, Bitter Betty, say one can only be a visitor for so long.

I enjoy escape routes that mark me as refined, such as shifting to Sauvignon Blanc at the first hint of spring. While in winter, you should know I used to drink only red, but have now decided to go only as low as an oaky Chardonnay, white, white, white, in even the deepest of freezes.[12]

12. My new senior colleague took my partner and me to a winery, near a bakery in the city where I would soon live. The day was cool, and the winery was a surprise. She said to the gentleman pouring that day, "These are my friends. They have exquisite and subtle taste and would love to try today's featured flights." Among one flight, there were two remarkable reds; in fact, all of the reds grew more and more rich down the line. I realized, then, that I'd reopen myself to red to be in her beautiful company, and to imagine what a fit might feel like. It did not have to do with love at first sight, or love at all, but with the promise of a vista, the sea, and the choppy white waves that look still from each far away view. When I said I would come for the food, she said, she would feed me. It had to do with sharing something that was planned some long time ago, and that we intersected around the ideas, mutual people,

I choose to write in "form" once in a while, to test my skill, to keep me on my toes, and as a sometimes formalist, I sweat sonnets to cast my accuracy, to challenge my ear & eye. My vision is this: I am good enough to capture the extent of the problem, its circularity, its condensed force, despite the potential of my language and its expansive girth growing in my rotting stomach. But what form to catch the stench?

I hold my art in my arm like a proud mom or dad, and spread word of its necessary dissemination. I am so proud. This means I will never be a problem. I will say, *I got this, I won that. I'm Tenured!* And the sound will reverberate in my body, or resound innocuously as the gliding car down the road, or the child screaming on the deck of the suburb, and in a room, which I case, then drift within.

Not too long ago, a number of forces in the job market led me behind a house to a converted shed that was, crazily enough, for rent. The "studio" was small, and a beige sheet on a rod cut across a cubbyhole,

---

books, places, politics, at that moment, it clicked. So it wasn't just the quality of the wine, it was the brightness, and the air of truly meeting, something not felt but ingested, tasted and lived. Add to this that the next day my partner came back in from getting the *New York Times* with another surprise, Adrienne Rich's *Tonight No Poetry Will Serve*, which contains the poem "Innocence," in which the poet writes:

. . . However it was done
And the folks disassembling
  from under the tree
after you snapped the picture
    saliva thick in your mouth . . .

A few lines later, the poem concludes, "People craving in their mouths/ warm milk over soft white bread." What are the borders between knowing how violence endures, if even the violence of continued exclusion, approximation towards belonging, and how to capture what seeps into the imagination through the body, the fit, its involuntary actions, its cravings, memory, and the need to eat and to return to some satisfaction beyond one's control? Rich's words meet my mouth, saliva (milky-bread) at the same time as the memory of that red wine (round and lingering), marking how fluid the limits of language, of how to encounter, how to enter, shift in the long history of violation, erasure, alarm, and how to sort out some approximation, distance and perspective from what and how one learns to enjoy, to finally taste.

its only closet. The view was a courtyard that revealed small cracks where grass shot up, and somewhere back there were some attempts at what the owner described as a "garden." None of this mattered, though, especially because despite how nice I was to the landlord, that I introduced myself by first and last name, and my partner in the same manner, he still said, "Really, I thought you were his chauffeur."

"Far from it," I said, but, really, how far? I choose poetry to explore the limits of a fractured self, always on the mend, or I write to see how the fracture looks within the assumptions of a shifting poetic stability, though I do often rattle some deep belly blues song, once in awhile, as it belies my complexity to balance in the same self that imagines at this point that it can say this, and looks out of the window into the memory of saying close to exactly that in the Skype screen where my background is constructed behind me, so in front of you, you will see a stack of neatly ordered books.

What you don't see is the shelf beyond the frame, books jammed up, others in boxes, some in a basement, and there, papers wag out, like dead tired tongues. Who do you see as you close in on the picture of me looking out at you, my design, so clean and clear, to say this is why I want to go there? This is why I want to be there, to say I imagine what you want, your needs, where I see myself, my own, in what I say and in who I am.

FORM

DRAIN

Where you are poison,
dig it out.

Where you have a dream,
you are where.

Where you want to be held,
open a window.

Where you wash,
open your self: *drain*.

FORGE

On a wire, drops and wind
sound like water flies from tread.

On the curve of a road, you look
into redwood. Hope no rope.

Alone, you run. What you get
through a screen: *a bird on a pole.*

On this asphalt mountain of mist,
what you forget, what you forge.

NIGGARDLY

A muscle, you oxygenate. The rain quiets.
You soften your eyes.

A gecko, camouflaged as a leaf in a forest.
You hurl it in the stream,

Voice thrown into the distance:
"Now can I use the word Niggardly?"

HATER

Your mouth is fake, so is "congratulations."
You hate her claim: a star, her friend.

You want her absent, not her silk robe,
a green annoyance, her hair, a red disaster.

You want to ignore her chewing. Her dumb play,
too. No. Fake it: Smile, smile.

HOW

One walks up and says, "so radiant,"
As though skin and hair, blind.

One walks up, should shut it. More coarse.
Be in his face. One should face it.

One sides up to the oldest with a bulge
At the table, bolted down: "This is the way."

Out his beard, one doesn't ask,
"Is this how?"

RADIANT

Do you work here? You feed funny.
You still.

Do you work here? Are you chef?
Are you maid?

Do you work here? You are a dot
in a field. Are you full?

Do you work here? You are so far,
how am I *"so radiant?"*

BLACK

Because you are black,
you can't cut the Saran Wrap.

Because you are black,
you can't know where you are.

Because you are black, you can't stretch.
You can't care less.

EXHAUST

Old, a proximity to black,
like if you'd called me old.

Old, a resin: no it's more like,
"Do you work here?"

Old, like you are old,
We'll both get old.

Old, we won't get black,
This won't exhaust.

I always tell my dancers: You are not defined by your fingertips, or the top of your head, or the bottom of your feet.
You are defined by you. You are the expanse. You are the infinity.

JUDITH JAMISON

Elizabeth Alexander in *The Black Interior* writes about beauty, and how black artists
resist monstrousness by their own self-definitions.

I'm interested in this repair, too, but find comfort in the ugly. I love monsters.
We both consider Brooks. In the poem, "The Life of Lincoln West," when Elizabeth

hones in on two white men describing little, black Lincoln, *specie*, I zip to the poem's
end, to what I read as Lincoln's release: it *comforts* him to be *the real thing.*

I align after June Jordan, *whom am I when pinched, patted, and bent*?
Get behind her defense of Black English in *On Call: How can I be who I am*?

We do with what's given. I suppose, I may not share viewpoints, but still,
I connect. Of prose, Meena Alexander says she uses it to clear the underbrush

to make space for the poem. Vacate fields, ropes, a body. Don't hate on Elizabeth.
Do you. Frame how she pairs Brooks with Lawrence and Bearden.

To argue, she opens walls, and living rooms. So, you like death? Is your project
Fanon's? Is this all a setup? Fan—on—it was a jolt in perception, then.

Pieces of this, repeat. Toni Morrison, where she reveals: *what remains were left
behind and to reconstruct the world that these remains imply.*

Ties to Brooks's litany of the black body that endures, a stream of violent verbs
to enter, under buzz and rows of halogen: *burned, bricked, roped to trees, and bound.*

Now, what contexts shift in the stacks that glare before you? And how do you return,
after, to what seized Brooks at Fisk, standing to face all those Blacks?

What was once writing about Stereotype
turns to elsewhere: I have this image
I can't escape. If I describe it to you,
you may lose your soup, or perhaps,
your bowels. What of torture?
Looking back from looking
at one torn open after the next.
Sometimes the body, hung upside down,
was severed completely in half,
but mostly, the crotch to head cut was slow,
saw stopped at the spine or ribs,
to prolong pain.
While the delineation of violence
is clumsy, the fact is, you translate
what eats you, and leaves you suffering,
something timely, something undone,
but to make the connection
from being burned, ripped, sawed,
and being constantly displayed—
I am looking into that, too.

On 20/20, a writer, whose face is bloated from binge drinking held on to both her prettiness and nerve to write a book about her college days as an alcoholic in Syracuse, where she got straight A's, but knows, now, she had a serious problem. Of course, I could care less about her looking out of her old self, montage showing the life she's lived, when I can't figure out this long road, or where I am going when I think about the black body's violation as an endless site of negotiation. How might we think of its constant flash of reiterative horror?

A corkscrew digs into the flesh. My escape into *Trading Spouses*. A rich "city-wife" is whisked off to a farm with her new family, where she tries to hold a Roto-Tiller that runs and beats wildly atop the earth and away from her, so that the son moves in to catch and guide them both: "Try this." "Try that." Maybe, I think I want to love this boy's helpful hand. But I laugh on my couch, which is not plush, or wide, but slick and brown and ridged with two thick throws.

The family sits down to eat "Clyde," the pet turkey killed by a truck. The son gnaws, "Watch out, that leg meat is tough." And the city-wife, who *would never eat roadkill*, loves the turkey sandwich though she doesn't realize. After the hunger has gone from her. After she's relaxed into a chair, and when she finds out what she's eaten, she's nauseous—scenes flash back: the turkey in the sink, the body in the bag, shots of the father picking it up, "right after it was hit." And the boy wanting to soothe his new mom: "He was still warm."

FOR THE SKY, IN WHICH YOU WILL ONE DAY, BELONG

You had it coming surely,
              Surely,
              Surely,
You had it coming surely.

"BALLAD OF PEARL MAY LEE," GWENDOLYN BROOKS

In this poem, a body is "gotten tomorrow,"
snatched, caught up—in these streets,
a chimp, firing screams,
ripping off a mouth.

Where did you get caught,
where you got caught?
In the face, you thought you had it all.
What will come is a door.

Open up. In your palm,
come eat at my table. What you see
is how you burn. Sometimes you
have to make up your own map.

Sometimes the body has to be told,
angle after angle, you are not wanted

to recall that when they sit around the tables,
your wings, they start to molt.

You realize, those birds are dead in the nest.
Those birds are dead in their fields.
The dark in your corner is in your corner.
Say, Convince, Cut.

The last image—its head split

did not want to think

of its shuddering

When you stuff in you the steel spigot, after you make the whale wash it
off with peroxide and bleach, you realize this is an identifiable limit,
a place where your body breaks as quickly as when
that same pig blew air inside you and forced gas,
unaware of how he filled your body like the water does,
where the green cove that's flat, moss and tires—
You ask, is there life there? And all the whale does is slather more
butter onto bread, and later, he will suck down a chocolate egg,
in a studio, and later still, he will make you stretch
out even though your face is too fat in the portrait of you he takes,
and now, you cannot button your shirt, you've eaten so much.
When he sucks out your ass, and eats your cum and makes you kiss him,
after, you hold back vomit, not like the "nigger" he said gagged on his cock.

The ants were smart to leave this artifact.

Forget the knife: forget the clicking in the glass.

The insect had no chance. It's split in half.

To do—let the bitch ant scurry around clueless.

Let the thorax and legs curve and curve around nothing.

So in the memory of it, the death speck sitting there, as if.

OTHER

Or character might be singular, plural, inexplicable, composite, evolving, non-human, or found.

ERICA HUNT

Under the car, it started with black rubber that melted into drops of blue flame
from the eight-cylinder engine onto Bond Street.

In the Chevron station, the cashiers are on the phone, before the large firemen dump
water on the chassis.

It will crack. My back tightens as my hamstrings extend, and I bend down to curl my
head into my locked knees.

The smoke is red, where the fire burns the paint, and the firemen are taking a long time,
while it engulfs the car's hood.

One fireman says, "I hope your insurance is good." I'm unafraid of his size.
Or his notes. I give him number after number as the car burns.

The outside of the engine blackens. Did I send a txt at the wrong time? The car slowed
down, and the gas didn't work. I got to the space, then I saw smoke.

As the engine's destroyed, my father loses his mind. He can make rice.
He holds for 20 seconds, then releases.

He says, "This is scary, babe" and I don't know what to say. "If you wouldn't freak out,"
—I learn to walk away.

My mom's Porsche gone in the fire, but it took me to the parking lot,
just like the blown tire of her Mercedes pulled me to an eddy on HWY 99.

I'm not lost, nor without the cash to buy a strawberry smoothie, and to find shade,
to get away from the heat until they come.

[MITCH]

You always wore socks and sweats, and made a fire, and you would not speak much, while we moved around your living room.

In it, I felt alive, and when I was there, I saw you last in that light. The air is cool now, in a room in which you've never been, and when I found your picture online, you and your friends at Candlestick Park—

The last time we fucked, it was on your couch, and you put on the Tranny porn, and I imagined your convalescing mother in the back bedroom, asleep, and remember, you said, "She eats good with me."

[RONN]

In the tiny hotel room, you look less like the giant I remember. Your gut, cool and curved like a big, white bloated frog's.

Outside of the window, the pigeons pace in the alley, and there's no wind. When I opened it, a black bug flew in that looked ugly between cricket and fly.

When we once went back to my apartment, humid, and you were soaked in your blazer, and you seemed to barely keep your balance on the train, but on that train, you looked at me and I felt lean.

Of that day, you said, you "balled" me. Remember, I would sometimes sit up late in your house, and look at the pictures of your life, you on the farm,

where you blew off your finger, and lost your eye.

I think about your wife coming home, appearing outside the sliding glass door, busting us. Her pussy, you said, sometimes smelled like urine.

[MITCH]

What you wanted was to suck and make me cum.
You wanted me to be a pizza boy, or ride me around in your Black Stingray Vette at night, or play pool with your friends.

I wanted to see you. I called, but there was no answer, and when I drove by your house in my mom's 928, the wheel was hard to turn in the cul-de-sac.

I know that was your brother, mowing your lawn. He looks almost like you.
I wonder now, if other men came around your house, your neat driveway and lawn,
close to my parent's place, only a mile or two away.

[LEN]

All I ever want is to open your belt, and to take out your cock
from your khakis. I like the way you eat lentils and nuts,
and keep things organized, clear, and clean.
In the end, I wonder if I called you right now, how quickly
you'd want to shoot. You love my voice—
I love your hairiness, but when I saw you in the city,
you were not as tall, and when I saw you at the beach,
you looked even smaller.

—you like to call me your pussy boy,
and I like to be called this, but so sneaky the fat caught up.

"Grandpa's gotta belly," and "I need cash," and you
 stuff a hundred in my front pocket.

I still expect it,
even though I've moved.

[MITCH]

Your teeth chatter when you fuck.

My teeth grind when I sleep.

You look at the DVD, rewind, pause, and look at the chicks
whose asses are round, whose dicks are big and fat and black.

Who do you have over besides me?

You're gone, but before this,
you finally treated my asshole like a pussy.

Spitting and fucking in it—

I even left wet once,
ate a Super Bird at Denny's on Mack.

July 15, 2011
8:49 A.M.

Dear Ally,

What can I say to the squirrel at the screen door, its back turned, springing off the step with its lower torso alive and darting? I believe in visitations. I believe that people can return from the dead. So, too, may animals, the shadow of your return, as consistent as that which passes my window. I know you're dead, but still, I blurt your name, "Aaaaaaaah/": The mouth opens. What I say to the squirrel is that it is a squirrel, and not a cat, nor you. How heavy you looked, black and warm on the asphalt. I wrote to Dawn to tell her you'd died, that you looked asleep in the street, and there was no blood, and this is what I learned today when I typed, "My cat was hit by a car," in Google. Many cats who go outside die. That outside cats have shorter lives than inside ones. I went to the sunroom where you liked to crawl on my stomach, kneading the fat that I cannot rid myself of, even after yoga, or running. I had a theory about you—this is that you were intuitive about my body, where it traps pain, and you would push away the knot in the shoulder or the pain in the base of the back, but what you really wanted was to touch my fat, all the places that felt good, all the weight I gained from that which I enjoy, you pushed. I knew I had to wake Dallas, to have him hold you in his big hands, hold you in a way I cannot. I wanted to, but I was afraid to touch you, your mouth still open after your last dying breath, the inside like Dallas saw, "all white."

Love, Ronaldo

July 15, 2011
11:42 AM

Dear Ally,

It's been six hours since I discovered your body. I want to tell you where I was, but I don't think that matters. What matters is that I did not let you in the house yesterday afternoon before I left. I know you realized this wasn't your home, but you always came over, and if I were not caught up in the rush of moving, I would have let you in to sleep on your chair in the living room, or the sitting window upstairs. Maybe the comfort would have been so enduring that you would have wanted to stay inside the night you would not have died, staying in when Dallas let you in after he finished in the hot tub. I was in Queens. I should have been closer; maybe if I came home a few minutes earlier, you would have seen me and ran up the driveway. Now, you will never do this. I'm at the Memorial Monument in Long Island, don't know the town, and I realize that you wouldn't care about this, but the tip, an obelisk, is so sharp and points to the sky. It is painted over with our flag, the colors wrapped around its body. I keep thinking of the time we were lying together, and you reached over, your claw tapped the inner corner of my eye, your eyes, iridescent green. You seemed to know not to injure, that we could stare, your arm my arm, my love, your claw. I realize all this brush they cleared around the benches near the flag helps me to see how you gave me what I was after when I used to come here looking for what I needed from big white men. Your body was different, your stomach, soft, and small, a place from which I could lift you so high, if I wanted.

Yours As Ever, Ronaldo

July 15, 2011
6:21 P.M.

Dear Ally,

In the hours just after I found you dead, I imagined your body wrapped up somewhere else. I felt you in my pillow. The pain in my leg grows worse, but I think I am coming to terms with what it means that you're gone. Judith Butler describes moving in grief: *that one starts out the day with an aim, a project, a plan, and finds oneself foiled. One finds oneself fallen. One is exhausted but does not know why. Something is larger than one's own deliberate plan, one's own project, one's own knowing and choosing.* Being in the world makes me realize that your death, and I think your life too, has humbled me into a kind of quiet. Maybe I'm just now learning about silence. I realized this when I bought your picture frames today, two, one for Dallas and me, the second for Mike, Mary Ellen and your real family. At the store, there was a mix-up in the price, and I felt the stress of the clerk maybe thinking I switched tags. As I looked at the sticker, it did look black at the edges. Remembering your body, how you stretched your arms into all of its length, I decided not to worry. I hear the cars speeding by. I'm not supposed to be angry at their speeding. I'm not supposed to judge the killer—I'm supposed to think that your killer may have felt sadness, too, after hitting you. Just now, light flashed along the floor of my living room, and I moved like you might have, whipping my head around after it. Today, I looked for your tiny little black hairs, and wanted you, here, asleep. I hope that you like the balsa wine box Dallas brought over as your casket. I wish we could bury you on the chair you loved, or with the warm summer night sidewalk beneath you. I hear the roots are thick where you'll be buried. Dallas said the boys helped to dig your grave, deeper, where Mary Ellen could not cut through the earth.

Below You Still, Ronaldo

July 15, 2011
6:47 P.M.

Dear Ally,

I don't want you to take this the wrong way, but today I was thinking of Apollo's death. We think he was part German Shepherd. One day when my mother went out for a run, she came back crying, holding only his leash. She looked so lost. Apollo was hit in the head by a car. Baby cat, his head exploded, my mom seemed to say with her lips, or maybe I imagined her saying it, but I don't recall feeling his death. I only remember not wanting to make my mother feel bad, so I did not cry, nor did I even let myself feel sad, or think I ever missed him. But your death is different. I hated seeing you lying there, dead. I wanted to shake you. I feel trapped, just like they say one is supposed to feel. There are many theories. One, we think you died from the construction that funneled the traffic down our street, so fast these cars move I can't even make sense of their shapes as they whip by, as though this were a freeway. You wouldn't stand a chance. I hope that you were lounging that warm morning, moving in your sleep, stretching awake, still in some almost dream, and the snap of your death like the sounds of the neighbor's hack into the roots, sharp and quick, like that, you went.

I Miss You, Ronaldo

July 16, 2011
5:32 A.M.

Dear Ronaldo,

Is your leg still hurting? I hope it isn't. You have a ton of work to do, and must figure out a way to move from NY to CA with as little drama as possible, but before I forget, what do you see in other men, besides Dallas? He's so warm and soft—I love his big hands, the way he held me that morning. I see what you mean, that he can love deeply, even in terror, and even in the space between sleep and being awake, a zone of animal feeling we share. Cats know this well. Remember when giovanni said cats signify the artistic self. I admit this is how I was able to enter your life. You'd be writing in the office, and I'd leap up on the window ledge, tap the screen, and see you seeing me, and my claws would open and try to hook in the mesh, but the glass was there, like the wood around the windows, like the wooden door behind the glass one, like the catch the door makes before it opens, the rub of old wood on old wood that lets me know, I'm in. You are in my heart—don't ever forget. Remember that I'd come over, and you never gave me any milk, or let me taste the food in your bowl. Dallas let me lick his egg plate, but we both know, he's different from you. He loves, unconditionally. I love that way, too. I think I know how you differ, but there's not much of this I can explain quite yet. It's just a feeling I'll never get to understand in real life, only in the memory of me in you.

P.S. I, too, loved the way that we last played in bed, the way you watched my claw open around the hanger!

Yours, too, Ally

July 16, 2011
9:43 AM

Dear Ally,

Do you know we buried you? Some people might think this is of no real consequence, that because you are not human, the funeral didn't count. Or because you weren't ours, it would count even less. Well, it does. In my office at my old job, there's a blackboard, and on it, I wrote in a thick, beautiful hand, *FIGHT FOR YOUR FORM*. It's from my dad who was talking about tennis, how when you're compromised, out of position, no matter what, you have to hit through the ball, your stance closed or open, your weight into the shot from anywhere on the court. What does this have to do with mourning? Perhaps it just means I am getting closer to what I thought I was getting at about my father, that my memory of what he said before he lost his memory is becoming more important than my need to remember him as I do now. I wish you were here as I sit and write this, but a fly is buzzing about me, and I think I am in the desert, and insects are hovering around your body somewhere. Dallas just came in from outside, and he usually doesn't interrupt me when I'm writing, but he did just now to show me a rose, single stem with three full blooms and a small one "for Ally," "Look at the thorns on this, have you ever seen so many thorns?" I asked him why he cut it, "for us to watch," he said.

Love, Ronaldo

P.S. My back is getting better—Dr. Diamond says, only do Bikram three or four days a week, and no-impact cardio while I heal. He suggests I buy Rollerblades.

XXO R.

July 16, 2011
9:55AM

Dear Ronaldo,

I miss the birds in the window, darting behind the lead-framed glass. I miss the way my coat got puffy in winter, and you'd know I came around by my prints in the new snow, the tracker in you, the love in my Dallas to clear the sill, the path below the bush, a trail from my house to yours. I guess I miss that you were always looking for me, and that I could run to you like that lion who was adopted as a cub by those two beautiful men. Remember when the lion got too big, and was released into the wild? The test was whether or not he would come back. So many years—so many kills, so many nights. I can't hear the music, but understand the feeling. Every day I saw you, I would come. You wonder if I had a special spot from my house from which I could see your driveway? Well, that's a secret! Just know that you always held a space in my heart, a wide field, connected by a stream of something I like to keep for myself, even from here. By the way, I was able to see my old body, and I did look really gorgeous in the wine box! I liked the flowers that Dennis and Eddie picked out, and the way Mary Ellen set me inside. I didn't look stiff at all—I looked so luxurious, even in death, my mouth soothed closed. Mary Ellen was crying when she closed it, I felt the hot tears from her face onto mine, the smoke from her mouth in my fur. Now you see where I came from with that smell that made you so mad! Funny, how I was wet and breathed on, like the way I used to treat you, dripping out of my nose onto your face and neck when I kneaded. I'll miss you all so much, how I calmed, and now bringing you all together with my still soft, black body.

P.S. Someday I'll tell you about my secret perch from Daddy Mike's house. But for now, look to the shadows of birds that cut above the hedges along the fencc!

All My Love, Ally

July 18, 2011
5:09 AM

Dear Ally,

Here is something only you'd understand, that I think I felt what you feel in a stomach just pushing back beneath a shirt. My fingers were cool against that fabric, my hands gliding around the surface, which was un-flexed, soft. You'd like the ride I'm on in the Limo right now. My body floats up and down, just barely. The road is smooth, and I'm not being shaken. I wish you were here, and it's so strange, because even as we get closer to JFK and the road gets uneven, winding, I still feel the touch of your body on mine. Dallas misses you too—he framed your picture and put it up in the sunroom—I feel like you're still there, and I know you're here too. I just looked up out of the window, hoping you'd give me a sign, and it popped out as soon as I looked up, ALLEY POND! We just passed it as we merged onto the Cross Island Parkway. I love knowing you are still near, the sky opening up this morning into a faint black, lightening to a purple. I'll keep looking for your signs!

Thinking of You So Much Right Now, Ronaldo

July 21, 2011
1:09PM

Dear Ronaldo,

I saw you today! I'm very proud of you. I'm not sure why I'm saying this, but it's the truth. I wish I could have told you this when I was alive, but I wouldn't have known until I saw you moving uphill, somewhere between grieving and something I can't quite explain. I don't have that kind of power. You do. All I know is that I felt your ease at that angle you moved upwards, your hip muscles firing, psoas muscle strained, still, you kept on climbing. This is what I meant to say—the deer you saw on the hill above Erica's house felt you, too, their heavy muscles, and hooves sure in the culvert between the gravel path and the woods. I saw you piss. You were so relaxed when you made it to that circle at the top. I'll never be up there, but how I travel with you as you find these openings in the world that lead you to where you once felt so zombielike, so lost. I wasn't surprised to see you return to the Memorial after you saw Dr. Diamond. Another man up there on the hill, the flash of his buttocks in the heat of the day, his cake-like mustache. Whiskers, like mine! You're so funny Ronaldo, your legs could barely bend, and there you were kneeling down in submission to someone who had no idea how to love. We all make choices. I chose, that night, to step out into the street. And though I could not hear the car coming, I could feel something heavy moving below where the pavement was pulled up by the machines, the digging that drew me even closer to the street, the broken rock and drying asphalt under me. I wish I could have heard it coming, and not just felt it, not because I could have done anything different, but because I would have experienced something new, just one more time. If I could hear, I wonder if I would have been able to soar as far and as fast as the deer that you saw today. Did I make sounds like that big one made? You thought, like sneezing, hard percussion, drilling into the air—did I ever sound like this when I leapt?

Forever Yours, Ally

MEMOIR

"I shall create! If not a note, a hole.
if not an overture, a desecraton."

GWENDOLYN BROOKS

SEA

I am lying in my bed, thinking about the space between my legs, this memory, attached to the hacking cough that builds outside my door. I wear earplugs, pulled them out of my head, from somewhere in my heart. There was a coastline, and I walked along it with my mother in a somewhere. I don't remember her hands, only the shelves of earth attached to the shore, as I held them. Guam is where I was not born, though I recall the urgency of the shore as if I were. A submarine is buried in the earth, standing above what's dead, perched atop a cliff. I want to enter this memory, but know that there's only rust built on the edges of a surface between earth and the useless hull, where what's left is locked and shut out of what I recall. Memory/Mode/ Move/Mill. Why do I know this about my body I touch? Where my fingers can't go I twitch—This is where I wanted an opening, where one is now closed, the zone between hole and soil, hand and skin.

An ant hill grows in a mound, near the landed submarine. The weight of it, like the cough, my mother's, or my father's in the bedroom down the hall, who says, "I'm OK. I got no memory, but I'm OK." I have no perfect recollection of this, and now, I think, like the surface of the water that pounds against the rocks, that red dust I kick in my flip-flops, is where I am tricked into kicking it. My brother, who wears shoes, is safe. They would eat the little boy I remember whole, if they could. Fire ants sting: "You look like a refugee," is what my mother would say to us if our jeans were split, shred at the knees, unpatched, our hair uncombed, undone by her wanting to forget all of it, her family, her language, my tongue. But she patches the knees, Green Lantern, Chicago Cubs, would fill in the ripped and worn.

I am lying between two men that I just met on Silver Daddies, one who looks like a fat grey god, though with denty-pocks in his skin not captured by initial digital profile, and he turned me onto his lover, the both of them, mine, my daddies, as I lose my dad to find these lovers, the soft belly of one in the night pushing against me, the squeezed sense between them, like a trigger I am trying to feel, to archive urge as a sort of continuous beginning. Where are the irregular fragments that break and shape us, those we make, imitate, act out and upon? We fit not. We do not fit. One daddy, Creamy Senior sends a note: "My hairy low hangers are wondering where you are. Stay in touch cutie."

I am sitting on another man, usually all of them are larger than me, and white, and not as refined as I am, even in the dark, my skin so smooth, I can't wait to set it against their dry flesh. Elbows wrinkle on those unreachable or inaccessible men, by job, by trailer, by trail that leads to one wife, or a partner reconciled to not being loved, so I grab a hand in the knock-off Apple store, a softness, where I expected firm. Ape tits below a Polo. At every turn,

The painter "takes his body with him," says Valéry. Indeed we cannot imagine how a mind could paint. It is by lending his body to the world that the artist changes the world into paintings. To understand these transubstantiations we must go back to the working, actual body—not the body as a chunk of space or a bundle of functions but that body which is an intertwining of vision and movement. [13]

A pointy Merleau-Ponty is this what I am getting at? In the weight of critique, the body, not quite, or almost—where's my strap-on? This writing into memory, sexual urge, as if this catalogue were possible, as if each gesture a litany of urges that begins with one border layered onto another, like the au gratin stack that holds the filet mignon like a trophy, or the bits of squid swimming in oil on my plate—all these bodies saturated into the next. "I am such a slut," she says in Tube Stack. Did Ruth Stone say that she avoided reading poets from fear

13. Maurice Merleau-Ponty, *The Primacy of Perception*. Ed. James M. Edie, trans, Carleton Dallery, Evanston: Northwestern University Press, 1964. 163.

of imitation, of being taken too far from her own voice? Maybe this is why when I am at my mom and dad's or with my Dallas, I watch *1000 Ways to Die* on the Spike Network. All the deaths are known. All the deaths are surprises. The water is different in the places from where I came. First, cliffs—I attempt a description—the wide ocean, or the deepest ocean, and then ridges set into waves. Mariana Trench.

Breathtaking. This assumes I put my fingers inside myself, or even thought of it, or wanted to put my fingers where, but I knew what I felt on a lap when I saw the skin lightly sprayed with hair, and the arm was wide, my imagined body up under it, and what you want is what I want. Let's just lie under the covers, and look up into the ceiling, like the Brady's, or let's get naked like The Six Million Dollar Man and his woman in bed, looking up. What do we say? What do we do now? I pour water into your armpit and it stays. No language to describe the desire, then, to capture what I set out to trace.

Television bodies bode, and build, and I am lying in bed wishing so bad at night that I had a split between my legs before something possible like "boy" and "pussy," like "boy-pussy" oscillating in the dark, but they were oscillating in the dark, not words, but like the strength of a riddle already solved and attached, like a remora to the roaming hammerhead under the ocean in which I was a moving coordinate, so it was easy to pick up the telephone to make a phone call, to Sacramento Overhead Door, or any place that had to do with Welding, or Machines, Car Parts. Their balls hanging low from their office chairs in the day, their wives, their lives, all given to me during my lunch break, when I got a pass to go home, leaped a fence to get to them. "Mom, Where's the SunnyD?"

Barbara Christian's *Race for Theory* comes out of the recollection that surfaces from this memory.

Variety, multiplicity, eroticism are difficult to control. And it may very well be that these are the reasons why writers are often seen as persona non grata by political states, whatever form they take, because writers/ artists have a tendency to refuse to give up their way of seeing the world and of playing with possibilities; in fact, their very expression relies on that insistence. [14]

14. Barbara Christian, "The Race for Theory," *Feminist Studies,* Vol. 14, No1. (Spring, 1989) 75.

My name on the phone to those men was Candy—don't forget this. It codes. It codifies. You can't. Where there is a line that has no origin, a too far away to remember, too small to feel is where you felt. I do understand I'm trapped, perhaps by choice, by what could be addictive desire, the need for repetition and recovery, seeking you in any way, like a first music I want to tear into, but I also understand that there is a wide river that I moved near, dark and muddy, a before next to the Mississippi, and the surface belies undertow, swirls from the bank I recall. There's also mud in the ocean at a depth I can't imagine, fluorescent teeth, spines. There are fallen arrows in Shelby Forest, too.

I lost a friend, recently. I still have his lamp and his clock. He was in sales. The lamp and the clock are in the storage unit marked, "J." He liked me wet, and now I miss him, but realize that he was incapable of sharing anything but his own fear and reproach. This I see in the pictures I took of him to put up online. The memory of the act of taking the pictures at that place is nothing like this bridge that I thought hovered between us. Two regular guys he might have thought. Why do you love me? Maybe I taught him how to love, maybe I teach them all.

Whatevs. Depth in desire, I give them something hopeful, a hole with no obligation, a brilliant dinner date, the wine is like gold or honey shot through glass. I give them dimples. I give them what they want. I take what I need, the pulse, the shoot, the heat. Am I looking for my father? He's here in the next room. I hear him hacking in the sink. He's cooking sausage, and I wonder when he will lose all language, his world, a world of notes, checks, when he ate, when he took his meds, when he will play golf. "I got no memory, but they're takin' care ah me." One of my daddies says to me, "It's really brilliant that you are mourning now, preparing to lose him. That's smart." I cannot even imagine the version of my father I miss, long gone, and the other is losing himself in front of all of us, and at this near end, I'll kiss any lips, open my mouth to suck the stranger's tongue in, without a care, an act I don't wish to name. What do you want when you say I love you?

This is to say, she says: *For me literature is a way of knowing I am not hallucinating, that whatever I feel/know is.* [15]

In Tennessee, a large concrete lot, and a shelf, and in that shelf, a coughing space, a spitting wall, a water fountain, the long walk between what I recall and what gets captured in a bomb shelter.

Do I feel distant from what I perceive as the critical project, or am I attempting to make sense of it as it builds inside of me into something else I do not expect. An essay? Maybe. Before I found what I was looking for, or maybe part of it, I thought I should read Barbara Christian's *Race for Theory*, again; and now I did, and I think I was mostly right.

That what I remember about her is us sharing an elevator, and her looking at me, asking, "Have you seen *Looking for Langston*? You really should see *Looking for Langston.*" So warm and generous, her curious knowing, her smile, the freckles on her smooth brown face. I thought this might have something to say about the heart of the imagination, the self, dropped from its signal, then recognized, but I found her call, opening me to the sea of what I didn't know about myself then.

Hydrofrac, Hydrofrig: 29. He sucks a beshitted ass, he has a tongue frig his own beshitted asshole, and frigs himself upon a beshitted ass; the three girls then exchange positions. [16]

15. Ibid. 77-78.
16. Marquis de Sade, *The 120 Days of Sodom and Other Writings*, Compiled and Edited by Austryn Wainhouse, and Richard Seaver, New York: Grove Atlantic, 1966. 577.

Farid, on our way to the airport, describes figuring out a way to understand his relationship to pornography as not pathological, and as I scan the service road for the adult theaters I passed on the way to the Belmont Hotel, he offers some non-pathological terms he embodies, *compassion* and *permission*, and that the ethics of one's relationship to one's love for porn must be fraught with both. That at some point, he wasn't going to police his desire to understand the pornographic makes me think of my encounter with the Marquis de Sade's *The 120 Days of Sodom*, a source text for me, a kind of exquisite creature of various bodies, an extreme landscape of possibilities shot across a moving sexual terrain that helped me to see what was possible in language, the impact of the clustered fuck (and other) scenes, their wild and impacted nasty brevity that marked my coming out of my unconscious relationship to the pornographic, my own sexual acts: on boats, in old hotels, cars, parks, the glossy old *CR* magazines, or *Daddy*.

The walks down 4th Street in the Village, or the turn off on the back roads to the big now closed theaters in CA whose names leave me, one woman being passed around from lap to lap, cock to cock, the glare of the porn in the background. The movies, to me, were only sound, the walls, cold, the men lined in the dark in rows, the stinking uncuts, where I sacrificed my breath, cleaned with my spit, to suck, and sometimes, a man was stolen from me by a true pig, cock-jacked, jacked cocks.

Sometimes a woman entering, one with a lover, and the infrared binoculars came out, then the men hovering around them, moving like a wave, or wind, a swarm, and I had enough remove to understand in these shifts of bodies in space, en masse, I was at home, but I don't know if I accepted it then, or understood the weight of what I wanted to see, this desire, mobilized into a where, a where that I could see forming, the place in which I could belong.

De Sade as guide, the act of reading him, pulling me out of belonging, my own loss between sound, my being pulled through the layers of quick language, the burying of one body, one head exposed, fuckers killed at the point of climax, a child, or a father, or mother, staring at one another, at the point of assassination, the language, a protracted performance, an elongation of desire, caught pain at the point of ejaculation on the surface of this or that zone of the body, or the candle, or the knife, or the carriages sweeping from one scene to the next, Libertine, Liberty, Let Freedom Ring, Free at Last, Free at Last.

Farid keeps one computer screen window open to porn while doing work on another, and describes the people in the worlds of his favorite amateur porn scenes that he watches, feeling them as if they are part of his family. It makes me think about the men I recognize on sites by simply the flash of their hips, the sight of their hands, their cocks, even if only for a second, the way they flash across the scene of what's become so familiar, them, also like a family to me, a family of beings, or signs, of impulses to connect with my need for them in my life, too.

Some men I return to, like Dick Nasty, or Dave Cummings, the way Dick likes to go doggy, then pull out and waste in the girl's mouth, and Dave pounds like an erect building, his cheap, faded elastic banded shorts slipped off, and the fact is, he can't cum that much, but the pour of it into a small, pulsed out puddle. And there are those with no names, the one when I searched for love, finds me finding him, kissing his wife. His white beard and the way they hold each other—maybe this is the love that I always wanted from what I knew wasn't possible, the familiar just outside of the reach of the real.

One screen open to the next—how to give the self compassion and permission to feel what holds, these men, my daddies, my desire, moving around the women that enter the scene, the wives, these women on their arms, the ease of their ease in being watched, the story, at least the one I think I need.

In the movie *Shame*[17], the annoying protagonist is not jacking off, but eating cereal, the streaming moaning in the background, while he is at the table made to look pathetic. He seems to always be running from his desire; in fact, I think, at some point, he goes on this long run after work, late at night because he has reached an end. It might be Montreal, but I do not care where this is, because the city is as unfinished as his desire, and on this night run, or maybe before it, or after, he goes to a gay club, and gets sucked, and another night, ends up being punched in the face, it feels like, for fagging out, for desperation, the accretion of the depicted addiction. There are some clues: A sister dies. Suicide. He hated her. What happened? Who cares—the whole while before, he jacks off like a rabbit to what seems like nothing, triple scenes, stark, the world his sex-box in triple cream, but so out of his reach, and for a moment, and maybe for all the time, before this ride to the airport, I identified and was only able to see my relationship to his pathology, the construction of it, as cautionary tale, vibrating somewhere in here, and then Farid says, at some point, on the ride home, we don't need another slim volume of connected poems, not another.

17. *Shame.* Co-Prod. *Film 4* and *See-Saw Films.* Dir. Steve McQueen, 2011, 101 min.

PUGET SOUND

It was all so very grey, the streets too, and the buildings and even the water from the 24th floor of the Renaissance Hotel, and so was your disposition, which was matched only by the weight of the clouds before I became soaked with my sweat. The Tortoise and the Hare—the long, loping runner next to me sets his treadmill to 7.0, and then strips his sweatshirt off, and resets, and I'm counting my calories to outlast his leanness. I go on where he is long gone.

I want to eat everything I can in the pantry before my mom gets home. I've attempted to capture how much I poured down my throat, Kraft Parmesan Cheese, or topped Beef Jerky on white bread, flooding my throat down with the filling enough so I felt stuffed. But what is writing about it?

Who are the witnesses to the self, and how do I crowd around the elements that mark this, that say, I was hot then, or hungry, and is this the same now as I look at the flight attendant's gut, and the slit where his pants couple into his ass, and he's old, so old and white, and his hair streaks back, and I want him to be my daddy right now, at least I say this, quietly, or feel this loudly. So that the fracture is that you'd do anything that walks by, the most simple, falling down to do anyone, bear, trucker, hairy old motherfucker, preferably light and orange or blonde.

It is not touching blackness, not touching whiteness, but understanding that it is about forcing something into the layers to get something out, to break through the rock of the psyche, then the rearranging of each fragment that accumulates into who you are at any moment. It is not resistance, but rolling with the microaggressions, one gesture next to another, unmoored, but I don't recall when I first called a lover Daddy, or whether or not I believed it when I said it, but now I say it to Daddies on couches in lobbies in airports, or hotels, or to those passing in the street, and for the first time I ask, out loud, "Have You Seen My Daddy?" I miss being unloaded of all of my cum on a bed or in a shower as a child, but think of the warmth of all of it over me, first sense, seeking the vision lost, the eyes not opening. Bukkake Eyes.

What I am attempting to do here is to find out how to speak each instance of my sexual being. I call or think of them as urges, to trace out where or how they accumulate, dart and dodge around work, productivity, the sentence, sense, what became such a pull in my life, the long line of it driving across every action. There are triggers. We know this. We are seen through the scrim of the fluid.

I think it was Sean Connery, but no, it was really Roger Moore in the credits before the film, or after, *Octopussy*, where he swims naked in silhouette in the ocean, and I wanted to only catch a glimpse of his dick outline as it danced in the sea and screen before me. Pre-Tube Stack!

I think the sun that draws across the horizon this morning is the light of my friend, Roman's death, burning in the sky, and he holds it, and I don't understand how he died, or exactly when, and the water moves across a wide field, and this opens up into a not knowing about the projections of the self that shifts, when you know but you don't know—Everyone wants to know. Tata is not telling. Some ask. No one answers.

I'm sitting on the fence that splits my neighbor's house from ours. Navy Housing. Shared yards. In the summer there are green beans that my mother plants, makes shade, a canopy of privacy, but it must have been winter when the wire gave way to the light of the sun, and the view into the neighbor's kitchen. I cut my shoulder open, there on a fence. The scar that remains, and grows. I think I remember him, how hairy he was, and I don't even recall seeing a cock, only the dark hair on a pale white man, who must have known we were looking in, or the aggressive hand of his wife, swiping the curtains closed to boys looking in, "My tee-ting gets hard when I see naked men." "My tee-ting gets hard when I see naked women," and then we looked in together.

Growing up, no one in my family wore clothes. It was like being in a sauna at all times. Sometimes there are ways to think about the past, but I can't point to them, and I can't think of a stage of being where my body collapses into one self that's sitting there looking through that window. What's left is a field, and being near a girl who sang, *fuck me, if you need someone to fuck to* . . . . in place of, *Call Me if you need some one to talk to* . . . . We were 11 or 12 and I had no interest in thinking about who or what she was, there, or how, or when, or whether or not my developing sexual life was connected to hers. Why would I care?

I met a child molester, who was convicted of the crime of molesting a 13-year-old boy, and he went to prison. He now has an older lover, and struggles to get a job. He was in radio. He feels, in other words, *poor*, but I do not, and when he fucked me, I thought here, again, is another one inside, but he's special. He represents what I wanted as a child, that man who I wanted, all my life, caught against the glimpse of them on the late night news, shadows carted off somewhere.

RAPE

The man next to me on the plane has brown nostril hair that juts out like thin spider legs. He swirls his can of Corona Extra in a circle as though it were the glass of wine I remember in the Napa Valley. Turnbull. He was a stocky one, the manager we met, again, down the road, at another winery I can't remember, and now he is swirling his glass on the table, teaching us how to taste the wine right. Aggressive. Swirling in a circle, the way his wine opens up and fills the air above his face. Breathe. Taste.

I feel so full of shit. The shit I feel full of has been extracted of liquid, and it feels so hard in me. I drank so much Vodka last night, a shot of Belvedere. These men are so fat in front of me. The cab driver last night had halitosis. I hate that stench, so I got dropped off early. I'm looking to get to my panel. It grows without me on it. What comes out of the body, what warps, and where are the intersections yet to be traced?

My stomach hurts—What I write has nothing to do with beauty. When my mind bent into my back after someone said that one has to work through it, as an option, I thought of Burke:

SUBLIMITY includes, besides the idea of danger, the idea of power also. Pleasure follows the will, and we are generally affected with it by many things of a force inferior to our own; but pain is always inflicted by a power in some way superior. Strength, violence, pain and terror are therefore ideas which occupy the mind together.[18]

18. Burke, Edmund. *A Philosophical Enquiry into the Origin of Our Ideas of the Sublime and Beautiful.* 1757. Ed. James T. Boulton. Oxford: Oxford University Press, 1990. 57.

What are the boundaries of trauma in Burke's notion of the sublime, whether they be intergenerational, specific or received, and what are the expectations of that trauma in relation to the body as one attempts to capture it? Some artists come to mind whose primary impulse is to field trauma, and to explore its elasticity, Pope.L's greased body bags, Schneemann's scroll, Dyson's floating white plastic. I keep returning to these works, as though this is some kind of desire connected to their meanings in a language I might replace with the word Torque, Torpor, Lassitude, Lasso—Yee Haw, Hee Haw—

I think somewhere in a poem I write about the field I grew up in between the military houses where I spent part of my childhood, that they are connected to one another by this field. In the middle is a playground. I don't actually think of this playground as "fun"; in fact, I think of it as a scene of terror, or at least, a site of reflection, where I could, or maybe I have in the past, rendered the park and its contents as a site of beauty, but in the end I think it's important to think about the field of all beauty as the site of possibility, but where did the terror hover at the horizon of my play? I remember now, writing about the razor in this field, and the brown substance collected on its inside edge, and knowing that it was something I wasn't supposed to see, feel, or touch. But for a minute I was alone with that found substance. I would think of this scene as different had I been cut, but the potential of being cut is where the memory becomes most exact, and that I had the wherewithal to not get cut, or to look at it and realize the history of that crud would be injected into what I would recall forever.

In that park, I committed assault, at least I think of it that way, if I recall it correctly, though I was a child of say 7, maybe 8. Why did I throw that thick, airless basketball into that white, freckle-faced girl's face? I could say I did it because it was the South, and I was a brown boy there, and that I recall being in the back of an old man's truck going somewhere, maybe given a ride home with a pile of black boys, and even though I felt different, I was one of those black boys ferried to my house up the street from the baseball diamond from which we were all delivered.

In Guam, maybe, I rode a bike down a hill, and was attacked, or crashed and got into some fight with another boy at the base. My parents told me to tell any boy's parents if someone starts a fight with you, or maybe they said that, or I learned how to fight at some point near the origin of that lesson, offense and defense, or offense as defense, or maybe it didn't matter—I sparred, took judo, and would drill with my father on how to break an arm, a face, a spirit.

Why did I pick up that ball, that was somewhere in the space near where that razor dug in the earth before I plucked it out? In my hands, the leather bunches in my grip is what I most recall. I don't know why I did it. In a way, we were becoming friends, this little white freckle-faced girl and me, right there in that park, that I realize was more like an eruption between families, lives drawn together through the tug of the U.S. Navy and how it brought so many of us who were so different together in that South, that Millington, Tennessee.

Maybe I pushed her on the swing. Maybe I was pushing her or we were talking, and the swing seat was getting closer, the pendulum more wide. I knew it would hurt. I knew that if I picked up that ball and threw it at her face while she swung toward me, it would hurt.

I was learning the basics of tennis then, and with the judo and boxing, I understood force, or the impact of what it would mean to use momentum in my favor and against the object of impact. It was like throwing a mass of rubber into a wall. It was like being in a cartoon, so the wastelands of Popeye were my own terrain, and her face was the bulging bomb of Brutus's chest, and it was like leaning into a forehand, a push, and then smack!

Whose trauma was that—I mean when she screamed? Or when I screamed, because at some twinned moment, I broke apart into a kind of hysterical crying too, and ran home, from the park to my house, where my dad wondered why I was screaming. I must have been hyperventilating when I told him that I threw a ball in that girl's face. Perhaps that site of shock, the stuttering, the out of breath need to communicate the act of violation was from the same place as when that white man laughed at me and sprayed me with a water hose when I attempted to "tell" on his son, who attacked me, in both cases, until I was left heaving.

The buzz of the plane around me is insistent. It requires a kind of work to write when it feels like the air is being sucked out of you, and the mountains in the periphery below you reveal the heart of the revelation. Sometimes when I am cuddling, and I don't know if this has any kind of recombinant relation to sex, or the act of fucking, or after fucking, I like to pretend to weep. I sense that maybe this is common, and this emotion is connected to that feeling, or an inability to speak when filled with terror. So came the fake tears, and the faux heaving. There is nothing particularly beautiful about this feeling. In a way, these are the kinds of thoughts that I want to query a Dad on a plane, who calls me "man," but I think that I want to put to him a series of questions:

"Do you like to weep, do you weep when you fuck, do you cry when you fuck, can I suck your dick until tears flow out of my eyes?" This is not crying. Claudia Rankine in her *Don't Let Me Be Lonely* writes about crying, about the division between the emotion of crying and the wetness of the face, as though the two activities are parsed out from one another. One woman after a reading of an excerpt of what I've written here said, "I was raped 7 times." What was included in the talk (was it de Sade) that triggered this confession? Was there something in the accumulation of scenes that inhabited my imagination that triggered my mind, a face being punished by a cock until tears came, the opening and pounding into this kind of seeing, where there is nothing but shutting down, shut up.

BLOCK

The word block is so very close to black. The word block contains the word lock. The word black contains lack. William Pope.L describes the importance of lack, as a way of being that could replace the very being itself—Displacement of the self as Enactment. He argues that identity is inscribed upon a lack, and he plays with the tension of thinking about the relationships that co-exist between the hyper-sexualization of the black male (violated, presented, remembered, recalled), his replication of it in a series of conceptual performances that lead not to transparent understanding, of "getting it," or being read, managed for your need, your maintenance, but instead, a multiply-split dichotomy, its being suspended at the point of capture, as a *hole/whole*[19], which for me represents a formal mode of inquiry I slip into, or at least follow, too, or move through, this position engaging with a space through which art, and art-making allows.

I bought a journal, or rather, a journal was bought for me. It's for a moment or two, painful to think of buying, when one has been bought, or sold, or the threat of this persistent long memory exists. The memory sometimes manifests in the random form of critique and correction, but of course no matter what you do, someone will hover over your shoulder at expected/unexpected moments, and you, at some point no doubt, will be corrected. In yoga today, you notice this correction, where the hips were seen to not totally open, and

19. William Pope.L, 'Hole Theory', in Mark H.C. Bessire (ed.), *William Pope.L: The Friendliest Black Artist in America*, Cambridge and London: The MIT Press, 2002. 79

the teacher asked you to open your hips wider, but this was before you were ready to do so, because you did not feel like shifting for someone else in your own body, in your own mind, to open in your own way within the space of the yoga instructor's desire.

Do you ever feel disproportionately rushed in a line, so much so that the last thing the whites behind you want (you are often the only one in these lines) is for you to slip out a blue card and to swipe for some small loaf of this or that, a tiny salad, lavender dish soap, or something else otherwise gluten-free, at least for that second, your time, they think, is theirs. In the end, you decide that you will exercise your slowly developing breathing technique, to take it all in, to drop your shoulders, and to go even slower into the positions *at your own pace*. You sign your name with the fat plastic pen on the screen deliberately, and think about opening up each letter to their fullest, despite the person's raging impatience building behind you.

The act of writing is akin to dance. *Fuck you. Fuck off. Fuckall.* The move from the body is also akin to the air pushing out of my mouth when I am running. The act is very far away from the image I tell myself to recall, the light when I soften my focus, which means to tighten my eyes with muscles that allow me to stare without blinking, causing the light to radiate outwardly in streaks, shards of it fracturing from the center of the bulb, so that the light is akin to a star flashing inside a room. The streaks remind me of the bright white marks on the starling's dark, feathered body, holding cake in its beak at the deck overlooking the harbor at Aldo's. When the teacher says focus on the smallest speck on the carpet, or the thread on your towel, I see Baldo's sweaty black trash bag that de-scrunches next to me on the rubber mat in the hot room.

Later I think, are my students closer to some pre-writing, some primordial sense, some kind of insistent feeling, an impossible zone, or are they just lost? Block is close to plank, and plywood. I know very little about cut wood, but I think of two-by-fours as field weapons spiked with nails, or balsa wood as disappointing when it cracks, the too-lightness of packaged wings, planes sealed in plastic, snapped together into the grooves before flight.

The planes we made were as delicate as the leaf in my journal, a white leaf from some tree I do not know, and the invitations I have to refuse are as ephemeral as my thinking while taking a nap. I am running away, driving away from the subject of the self, maybe as a means to get closer to it—Sleep engaged with enactment?

Block is related to Bag. Pope.L puts one over his head for the cover of his retrospective's catalogue. I want to go to the Watergarden today, and relax, get fucked, but I have to, instead, go to a party. I might say that I have flown in late, and that I cannot attend. "My body is overtired," I will say, and the work week will start soon.

What do I seek? I look for something close to love and realize I can find it for $35, and get filled. Maybe I feel fulfilled. I am a poet. I am not a therapist. I am a black pot. I am a pot that you may not want to enter, or you may want to, in the end, but ultimately there will be something of the recognizable that is fixed, a body through which you will want to remember, or to think—My hope is that I'll go.

THE WHITE VAN[20]

The Zody's parking lot is not empty, because it's circled by a wobbling old white man who shuffles in the dark cooling heat of the Sacramento summer, and this is the old Florin Road, where there are no fences that keep out the transients that might climb over the fence into an abandoned lot. I'm driving a 1980 Honda Accord, tan, with sheep-skin seat covers, a black bra, louvers along the hatchback. When Donaldo would fill the back of the car with the tens or fifteens, it would rattle the slats on the dam, and shake the windows and the street. An Amp. An Equalizer. There are girls dancing next to us. Some would call them mud ducks, and, once, when one got too close, close enough to expect a lift, like Damita, he hurled a pizza box at her face and screeched off.

I am near a pond, and the pond is breathing frogs, a breathing I have not heard before this very moment. The breathing is hard to locate, maybe, like the laughter that begins behind me. The heat in The Berkshires is so different from the heat in Sacramento, and the bugs here, attack the body, so much so that my calves are snapping back in the heat of the memory of being so bitten. The van is like the moon this morning, flat and low in the air, and it's cold, so freezing in fact that I am shaking, not from the cold, but from the expectation of what I was about to have even though I saw it only on some video, how I learned to bob my head, to bobble like a good cock-sucking girl, the only rhythm found through this kind of repetition, something that existed so far out of my control, but it was a control I immediately mastered once he let me in.

20. "The White Van" was first delivered for the panel, "The Brazen Truth: Dangerous Nonfictions" for the *Litquake Off the Richter Scale* Conference, California Institute of Integral Studies, San Francisco, CA, October 7, 2012.

I think I said, "Excuse me, I've never done this before, but can I suck your dick?" And while asking I ate from a bag of chocolate kisses, and licked my boy lips at the old man, a walking fantasy, bobbling in and out of what felt like a dream. "A young man as handsome as you, you should be out chasing girls." A young man like me was out chasing after something out of his reach, until that very night in that cooling heat, chasing after the shift in the car, when the old man slides back the curtain in his white van, or slips out from the van, and then asks me if I want a beer, and I don't remember drinking the beer, only sitting in his front seat and thinking his cock looked like a big button.

There is a tray in the car, but I do not recall anything in it, only the stack of what had to be moved, before we slipped in the back. I felt out of practice, out of practice in something I'd never done before, out of practice in what I wanted to do for what seemed forever. Is this what I was waiting for?

Once, driving from San Diego to Sacramento, somewhere in the "Grapevine," the bra slipped off of the car, and slid under it, the drag of it slowing us down, pulling as it caught below the bumper. I don't remember if this was coming or going to Sacramento, but I do remember me, Donaldo, and my mother, in the car slipping under a bridge, flipping 360 degrees around, and ending up safely stopped under a bridge after my brother fell asleep. Somehow we all woke up under the overpass, and I remember laughing. We all laughed as a response to our survival.

In the pocket of the Van, there is a nail clipper that the old man uses to clean out his ears, which he likes to dig into. When he sees the young boy driving in the parking lot, there's something that he can feed from, something that he takes. Did he want to suck? I do, and there's his underwear, pulled down, and there's the spread of his thin, white legs. And he wants to try it. Does he say that? It's hard to sort out that moment, because it was so fast, but the smell remains, the smell of sweet beer and dead skin under the nails, blackened, the beard, so rough it scrapes against my face, and the space is so small, almost too much so, to hold these blockish movements, the hard shifts, and the softness in which I learn to track this smell as a first smell. The pull of it follows me. The soft white body—he is so rushed, and I am leaning into the sweep of his speed, or I crouch back to let it go by, does he offer beers? Or I run from them, I watch him explode all over the place, and the cum fountain in the dark in the van feels like this is the site where I am born, and I move in the van as if in a womb, before I break back out into the night.

THE BELGIANS [21]

William the plastic surgeon is bald, and tall, and he wears a gingham shirt, and he's thick and full, like his lover Patrick, who is in finance, and is also thick and full like him, so it makes sense they are a couple here at the Porch Bar, repetition of fabrics and length and foreign bodies, and foreign cocks in America. A man with a mustache is able to pull all of the men in the bar in. What to see out of the light is not clarity, but the pocked face that fills the surface of the street you walk out into, and despite not knowing where to go, you are leading, or maybe you are led like them all after this into it, dodging how to think of the split in time, place, and event.

The blacks are in front of the Marc Jacobs store on Commercial Street. You would think, like their borrowed makeshift photographer does, that they want to be seen together. Instead, they are attracted to the distance that spreads between them enough so that the name of the designer links them on the bench, where one sign creates reality, two brothas hitched by class signage. I do hear an accent, and feel resentful of their very presence, and need some stability. And when Dallas asks, "Who let them in?"—and even though I, too, feel this resentment, I say, "They are more beautiful than anyone here in town." Do I believe this?

There is a bird that moves across the sky at an angle, much like the way that I swim against the current, pushing myself, swimming below the waves, and despite the back hurting, and despite the bruise that grows

21. "The Belgians" was delivered for the panel, "Rewriting America: Race and Re-imaginings in post- 9/11 America," *Litquake Off the Richter Scale* Conference, California Institute of Integral Studies, San Francisco CA, October 6, 2012.

from the fall down the stairs, I am ready to continue my kick below the torque of the weight of the black men on the street in a pack in a white town. The white girls that slip by have no idea that I paid close to fifty dollars to get this seat, and I chose air instead of enclosure, but like Drake says,

"They know/they know/they know."[22]

With my finger holding in the stitches, I thought about the Belgians, not that I will ever see them again, but I want to call one "Prince Patrick," and the other I want to call "Lord William." They are so critical of black women's bodies, the shapes growing so wide, but they love Michelle, and their bodies are lean like Barack's—Is that why I made the wrong turn, the space between sleep and disaster pulling me down the stairs, a kind of freedom to be thinking in a house next to a sea. Who would have thought this would lead to laceration, the flying pizza, laptop, and the fall? What does one say, and how does one feel the slip between the act of encountering critique, and the idea of reaching through the repulsion of such naming, like the black plastic bag that spins below the grey jets that thunder outside of my Hilton, how dare I get so classed, and pulled over for such speeds down a hill to get to you?

They describe themselves as "elite," or above it all, or something that they can't colloquialize. This is a position as tricky as the one they describe as so difficult to maintain in the Gay World. They don't use that phrase, but like the bruise that grows hard on my hip, we both understand what they mean when they pass for "straight" around the world. In fact, we are linked by our very shirts—mine is reasonable, Ted Baker, not as cheap as I thought I pulled on for the hunt (I usually wear J. Crew), but the blue, 4, tailored down the back, two inseams to bring the body back in the shape against that which I gorge. I bought this shirt near the growing Twin Towers, my encounter, what I want to say, leaning out of windows, breathing in the blast. You know, there were days back then, where you could get a free air conditioner. There is soot, or a place where the body slips between class, outside of buildings, and in the end, all I think of is what has changed in the erection of the towers that grow below me while I vacate.

22. Drake, "Headlines," *Take Care*, Young Money, Cash Money, Universal Republic, 2011.

LACERATION[23]

Khary describes a series of men he met in Germany who all had black boyfriends that are now dead. One jumped from a window, and when his friends explained that they had to return to the apartment to clean up the mess, Khary, like anyone else, or at least anyone like me thought to ask, "What was left to clean up?" The answer becomes a punch line:

He slit his wrists before he leapt.

When I returned from the $138.47 cab ride from Hyannis to Provincetown, after getting my finger sewn back, ignoring the fact, or at least trying to ignore the fact that I was not in a Town Car, I did not expect to return to the pool of drying blood at the base of the stairs, the blood on the walls, the blood seeping from the washcloth, the slow rinse from red to clear. The caked blood on the faucet in the bathroom, more dried on the back of the plastic door knobs. The streaks of blood on the light switches, the faded splotches on the white walls where I tried to clean up after my accident, all remained, if even as spectral.

23. "Laceration" were first delivered for the panel, "Rewriting America: Race and Re-imaginings in post- 9/11 America," *Litquake Off the Richter Scale* Conference, California Institute of Integral Studies, San Francisco CA, October 6, 2012.

Climb up/ an escalator slowly/ ready to greet a room/
that you have no patience for.
There's one/ who says you look like Tracy Chapman,
There's another/ who says you are duplicitous/ who says you can't repeat
your name/ who says the name is understood/ who says the name is undone/
who says the buildings are crumbling on the television screen in front of you/
and just down the road, and just where you were, and just in the trap/
Wall Street Sauna, old men are piling against the steamers/ this is the decline of
something/ you go to Les Halles/
you walk across the street/ it isn't quite pain, but embarrassment to move up that/
freedom tower/ it isn't quite embarrassment, when you look down,
and see the reflections in the pool.
What is the reflection in the pool that you're looking across—
across the vast distance of memory? How do you sort it all out?
Have you gone so clear? You remember these things.
You are sitting on a subway platform/ you are waiting and waiting
and what normally takes two hours, takes five, or seven.
They are walking across a bridge. You are deliberate in your waiting.
You tell them, don't wait outside. You tell them/ don't go outside.
You imagine planes bombing the city.
You revert back to earthquake training.
Get under a desk. Get under a table.
What you enable is hunger. It's what the split happens when it falls.
Desire's collapse. There are buildings. There's something building inside of you.
Is it stress-less? Is it sex? When you were on the subway platform,

What would trigger you is a chin or a cheek,
any beard or glasses, or old man/
There was a point when you let your pinky extend to touch him.
Or, you lean back, looked for perverts on the subway, sherbert that you ate,
It's perverted/ the subway links like the cars are slowing down.
You're deliberately waiting. You're trapped.
There's nowhere to go in this traffic, but to think back.
What do you remember, post 9/11? Close to the instant,
you and Dawn Martin at the scene of the crime, ingesting/
body parts, fumes. The fallen lover's stomach is falling out/
and the eye is bleeding/
and the finger's been blown off/ and the memory is gone/
and nostalgia holds that realm, that resin of what it once was, what you were
climbing up that hill. Climbing up the stairs, or waiting for the elevator
when the music would start. You associate death and sex at that moment,
post-apocalyptic. The men are beautiful that slash the faces, Jen says.
The men are beautiful in their razors.
Tazered on the block, the television is blacked out.
It's fuzzy, it's hazy, there's nothing but a crane.
Everyday you turn and you see a crane,
And you look at the sky, and you see the smoke,
And you go to work and your boss's boss's boss's assistant
takes a bike and says classes are cancelled.
They want you to teach the Harlem Renaissance.
It's not your field or area, they throw you a class,

You want a bone, you get a better job.
You get a fellowship, you win a prize/ you distance yourself,
you have to defend your self/ you have to defend, why are you thinking this,
post-apocalyptic scene, 9/11 you're there.
What are the consequences? Freedom. Operation freedom.
We will/ blow them away. "It was an explosive year."[24]
You remember Samiya Bashir saying this: Recount the poem.
It's only in the imagination to be stuck in the traffic, you're just moving slowly,
the break's likes should be soothing.
The brakes's lights should be enduring,
          enduring freedom.

You're walking with Rori down somewhere in the East Village, nope
the West Village where you once lived, you got off at the subway.
It's as though you're returning to the wound and you're singing,
and you're looking at the posters, and you get as close as you can.
She's turned on by the firemen, I'm turned on by all the paper/ all the missing.
All the missing units, this isn't photo collage/ there's no direct feeling,
but when someone throws a backpack on the ground,
everyone's ready to launch.
It was the first plane ride that you took,
and you landed at applause. You owe your father money.

24. Although I remembered hearing this line, as such, when I heard Samiya read (I think) at the Schomburg in Harlem, my line is improvised from the actual title of Bashir's poem, "The President's Explosive First Year," which appears in the chapbook, *Teasing Crow and Other Haiku* (New York, NY: Sistafire Publishing, 2002).

He says, "Where's my money?" You say my city was blown up.
You say, I need time to adjust.
How do you look back at this time, at that instance?
Do you feel more or less/ under siege? It was before/ you were under siege.
"We have always felt this," at a talk once. Lucille Clifton and Sonia Sanchez said
—they were the ones the day after—"There is potential/ in all humans for great
good, as there is potential for great/ evil," is what Lucille said. I don't remember
what Sonia Sanchez said, but I remember that it was something
about we've always been under fire. There was a certain amount of joy, I felt,
at the/ unleashing of something in a city, where one walked and one feels safe,
or where one feels unsafe, for instance, when I got off of the subway, on my stop, I
would run, with my new laptop, because I knew if I walked, I'd be a target/
who would try to catch up?

Sometimes I walk slow if I have nothing in my pocket and say,

what/
is/
up/

in some kind of cadence . . . .[25]

    Scare, scar—they feel so close. My hand is wrapped, but after the laceration, my sister asks me to write a story. I don't know where to begin. I don't know how to bring the self that I felt breaking down the stairwell,

    25. Ronaldo V. Wilson, "Post 911 Reflection," *Off the Dome: Rants, Raps, and Meditations.* Sound Recordings. Unpublished.

one surrounded by two foreign men, moments before, then on a bed. Throat drilled.

If this were *One Thousand Ways to Die*, the episode in which I would die might be called, "Pizza Party Peril."

"After a night where this Lothario picks up two Belgians Daddies at the Porch Bar, gets it in, and after, gets a few hot slices to celebrate . . . " You don't finish the story. Pus indicates infection. I have a rubber glove in my bag in the case that it rains. My laptop, even though I fell with it down the stairs, remained intact. What do I have to give? I tell him that I could fall in love with them both. I say, "I could fall in love with you," into his eyes, and he says, "I am complicated."

When I see the Belgians at the bar the next night, after I have fallen, after I have returned, I point at them both as though we are on a fútbol team, and one of us scored a goal, or they are far away, and I am pointing to some realm of knowing reserved for men. I was chasing something. I cannot get hard for them, and I think it has to do with the way they do poppers, and how one leaks from his eyes. I slip my hand over his face. I try to get him to somewhere else. This is before I have fallen, before I am stitched, before I am splinted.

I wonder what Candy looked like to them—I tried my best to describe her as small, and because I was maybe 12 or so, or just turned 13, I had near zero baritone in my voice, and the reaction to understanding who she looked like was connected to the lie of her existing in my voice in the first place. I think I said I had long dark hair, and tried to sound thin, maybe revealed my real skin color, hair down to the middle of my back. What would a boy know? Do I misunderstand the site of the lie, now? Does the lie inflect itself around the need in wanting to get fucked before this could be imagined as possible in my own body, or the risk in knowing that I then, pre-caller ID, could be traced *69, and sometimes was, a call back caller shouting, "Who is this!?!?," and I would not answer, and nor would Candy. We, in an instant, could both be not there.

Perhaps I am comfortable now, in language, because of this lie, the exercise in working between the lie and the amorphousness and control of that body connected to the possibility in this collaborative fiction, me, with this other, the choice in designing the receptive self, serving as a space in the imagination where who could become could also be radically undone when my mother came home, say with her friend, Nebraska, the house scent-rich with my boy cum—"What's that smell?," and I said I made some clams for lunch, something I don't think I ate, or I may have even said I made oysters, also something I had never eaten then, and wherever would I get them was forgotten as they cooked lunch, my mother showing off by making steak.

At the Belmont Hotel, they are so beautiful these lovers in the window left open as an obvious display, and this beauty is tied to a kind of thinking that presupposes the sun that must frame my face, that can also be seen against the headboard, especially if I prop up the pillow. I think to myself, maybe I can blend into it, though I realize I am not as dark as this varnish, but I think if I lean back, I am actually dark enough, dark enough to camouflage myself into this room, entire.

Maybe I can look into the self as a wall, a way back, into and not being seen in the room where I am? They, too, pull the blind closed, just enough for them to be shrouded by the sun and its shadows, where I can see their figures through the window. They realize, I am fairly certain, that they have shown it all, her bob, her kissing him, a grey head and large cock, him playing with it behind the MacBook Pro screen, the bitten off white apple, logo that both calms and blocks my view, though I can see his hands jack, and she reclines, or lazily expands in the show, here in the room, then there, and I am hiding out of sight looking in and at, but pretending to be writing, or maybe I am writing, or looking as if this is so, then I will get up in my yoga shorts and stretch, to feign my glancing towards them, then at an angle away.

At dawn, on a street I do not remember the name of, I am in one of my customer's yards, and this is pre-Candy, but full-on Paper-Boy, horned up and looking into windows, seeking men before they go to work. I move back and don't notice one pulling the blind back. Nothing is said, nothing spoken, and I'm driven by Spivak a bit here, where she describes the possibility in the subaltern's consciousness, and how this is caught . . . . *The sender—'the peasant' is marked only as a pointer to the irretrievable consciousness. As for the receiver, we must ask who is 'the real receiver' of an 'insurgency?* . . . .[26] This is not a history, and I do not quite know how to mark who is so named as the pointer or the one pointed toward, but I did feel like I needed some way to mark who I was in my desire for whom I knew I could never have, the mystery in figuring how to mark the space between us.

If the man on my route readying himself for work came outside, after busting me, my lie was that I would say that I threw the paper in the bushes, that I went to retrieve it, and got curious. And when the curtains parted, and he looked out to see me, he just shook his head, "No," and looked down at me. Nothing

26. Gayatri Spivak, "Can the Subaltern Speak?" *Marxism and the Interpretation of Culture.* Editors Cary Nelson and Lawrence Goldberg, London: Macmillan, 1988, 287.

happened after that, no call, no communication other than him above me, and me feeling a coolness in my chest, an open feeling twinned with the morning air.

The Prank Call. The Peeping Tom. I was also the Bike Riding Boy on his elementary school grounds, riding between the classes and bungalows, pulling his pants down to ride in the school, my naked 6th grade asshole on the BMX seat, the paper carrier bag draped on me, and my cock out, long and hard into the fresh blue light.

And as I look out across the windows, I am also looking, as a boy, up, and down into another man, and his lover, through the events rendering me alive, and at the same time, in a way sexually useless, inert in my movement, so that when the couple appears in the lobby, and the daddy says "Hello, how are you?" and the wife does too, I am unable to act beyond my own, "Hello, how are you?" all of us as neutral as we are aware.

THE CAPTURE OF SAMANTHA PHAM

Samantha Pham "The Sweetheart Swindler," who took my father for $310,000, when she wired the money to a shell company that "dissolved after the transaction," looks like an Asian blow-up doll, bright red and blue make-up in the photo, her face on KTVU.com. She's caught, and the report, which details her brown and pink prison garb, and her looking down, shaking her head after she is trapped in that jail, matters not to the house in my father's imagination thick with regret so heavy that I think it's slowly killing him, cell by mind, loss by cell.

We'll never get the money back, but my father has shut all this out, perhaps his dementia, taking him far from the realization that everything he worked to give us, he understands now to be gone, gone to Casinos, a room full of expensive luggage, an autistic sister. Wherever. Among the other victims, his name is the only one used in the article that says Pham is in jail on $1 million bail, because the DA in San Jose was given leads to a trail of several elderly men and women who've lost some $3 million or more to this Sweetheart Swindler.

I think it was somewhere around this time, when my father was making sure his investment was intact, the money not coming through in his fantasy 25% return, when sometimes, I would go downstairs, and my father would be jacking off in front of the television, a feverish action, tight, quick, frantic, a being outside of himself, someone who I always knew to be so secure and solid. "Whaddyou care?" This is what he said, when we described what others thought of us.

How do I return to that floating moment?

Once when I rushed down the stairs, and I "caught" him, and ran out to the garage, he popped up at the washer near me in a few seconds, where I was the one shamefully filling it with my clothes. We said nothing to one another. He looked at me as if to say, I cannot tell you who I am, what I know, what you saw, but there was something in his eyes as if upon the threat of food stolen, meat snatched back to the mouth, in a car, a corner, a cave. The events are not in fragments, there is simply this one scene; it leads along an emptiness, a field, always open, and maybe this inability to close it is somewhere deep, and now, in attempting to hold the scene in view, reveals what's connected to this dream where I am to meet my father with my mother at a restaurant where I've never been.

Dallas was in the dream too, and in it, he told me that my dad has been picking his face until it bleeds, and so when I show up at the restaurant, and I am late, and hungry, and I still have time to order, I am shocked to find my father looking healthy and beautiful and not picked, bloody, nor scarred. His face is round, and he's full. He is shiny.

He is playing a game at the table, one where he is reading poems, first the titles, then the poems, themselves. One poem is called, *The Exercise*, and for some reason I goad him. I tell him, that this is the poem's title, but he tells me he doesn't know what a title is, and I tell him that I am showing him what a title is, and I say it to him, meanly, as if he were stupid, and I wage another attack: "This is exactly what this is, *an exercise.*"

My father explodes. The explosion is where the dream weighs heaviest, and it tells me that there is some relationship to this goading and my losing him in life, in dreams, in all aspects of how I will ever know him, our fight in my unconscious, the silence I keep as he fills the garbage disposal with spit, and wipes his snot on his sweatshirt, and how he licks his fingers, and cleans his dentures out, eating the food from its teeth, picking at it and licking out the kernels of popcorn when we took him to the movies. Horrid. I don't feel I can control myself, so I say nothing, or say, "Stop it Dad!" far enough out of earshot that when he answers, "What?" I don't respond, or I tell him to quit under the blare of the television upstairs, so far away from him that he would never hear.

My father screams at one point in the dream: "I don't know, I don't know, I want my Grandma!" Wet with sweat and spit, and in the next, "I Hate You!" As far as I know, my father has never seen a therapist, nor has he ever fashioned, at any point, his need to see one. "I have a bad memory," is not the same as his saying, "I am depressed," which I don't think I ever heard him reveal. At first, when the dementia began to settle in, he would flash and snap; and at one point, he screamed in my ear when I was dead asleep to wake up right then, to take a car to a shop way across town—"Don't signal, just get in front of them! If you signal, they'll speed up!"

My mother was starting to say so calmly, "He's getting senile." And my father: "This is scary, I feel so scared," and he would describe how it's so hard to lose your memory, and before that, he pounded his head against the wall, and before this, he passed out on the street, blacked out, crashed cars into other cars and guard railings. He put one man in a wheel chair, forever, and was taken to court to be sued. On the stand in the courtroom, he did not repent. Instead, he repeated, "I don't know," to every question, but when it was my mom's turn to speak, he laughed under his breath, then out loud, like a mischievous child—the letting go of life into the world of cracking up under it, one layer of the self released into never again recalling what happened, just the memory of my father, sitting on the curb, a galaxy of glass, the fence, bars bent into the shape of the van.

The consequences of being removed from who one was, into a beyond remembering, or at least caring about it, slips into the rhythm of a life: BLDW (Breakfast, Lunch, Dinner, Walk) /GOLF/JIM and the other old men who take him to play, and his long walks around the hood, and his pies, and this is what makes him happy and what keeps him mostly in our world, how he counts out his MEDS, how he longs to go to the store, whipping out to the car with a measuring cup of cooked oatmeal, or eggs and grits, or my mother covering the refrigerator with pictures from a life before this, one, me and my father, in the snow in New England, my boots, my then new car, and he's fat, and full, and I am in a black puffy vest.

"I love you! I love you!" is what I yell back as he screams how much he hates me in the dream, and as I hold him, and as he moves closer, he begins to suck on my nipple, and tries to feed from me, and I realize how small, and black, and hurt he is, how he is sucking for his mother, his grandmother, and I am not them, refuse all of this as I force myself to wake.

I am close to the dream when I am in the shower. What returns as I wash is when he told us how he was "hazed" when he retired from the Navy. Or maybe it was when we were transferred from Millington to Alameda? I'd never heard the word "hazed" before, but he told us, they put a Baby Ruth bar in a bowl with lemonade, and they made him eat it, and there was a blindfold involved, I think, and for every moment before this moment, I did not fashion that they made him eat out of a toilet. I thought there was an actual bowl, or maybe when he said bowl, I did not think of the toilet, but something else, something far away from that scene that held and marked the transitions between his job, one life to another, a story that he felt he should describe, and to tell his family, then.

ENDNOTE

Direct quotations from authors and artists appear as follows:

"If the terrain were familiar, the poem would be dead on birth." Stanley Kunitz, *The Wild Braid: A Poet Reflects On A Century In The Garden* (New York: W.W. Norton & Company, 2005). " . . . I become identical with the artwork, and the sequence is shortened . . . " Adrian Piper, 'Talking to Myself: The Ongoing Autobiography of an Art Object,' *Out Of Order, Out Of Sight, Volume I: Selected Writings In Meta-Art, 1968–1992* (Cambridge: The Mit Press, 1999). "Or character might be singular, plural, inexplicable, composite, evolving, non-human, or found." Erica Hunt, "Notes for an Oppositional Poetics," *The Politics Of Poetic Form: Poetry And Public Policy*. Ed. Charles Bernstein (New York: Roof Books, 1990). "I shall create! If not a note, a hole./ If not an overture, a desecration." Gwendolyn Brooks, "Boy Breaking Glass," *Blacks* (Chicago: Third World Press, 1987).

The original drawings and watercolors from the "Bear Gulch Diptychs" appear as follows:

Wilson, Ronaldo V. *Untitled (Drain)*. 2005. Artist's collection. Santa Cruz, CA. Ink on textured paper, 6.75 in. x 7.125 in.

———. *Untitled (Forge)*. 2005. Artist's collection. Santa Cruz, CA. Ink and watercolor on paper, 9 in. x 12 in.

———. *Untitled (Niggardly)*. 2005. Artist's collection. Santa Cruz, CA. Ink and watercolor on Paper, 9 in. x 12 in.

———. *Untitled (Hater)*. 2005. Artist's collection. Santa Cruz, CA. Ink on textured paper, 3.25 in. x 4.75 in.

———. *Untitled (How)*. 2005. Artist's collection. Santa Cruz, CA. Ink and watercolor on paper, 9 in. x 12 in.

———. *Untitled (Radiant)*. 2005. Artist's collection. Santa Cruz, CA. Ink on petal and leaf paper, 6.667 in. x 6.667 in.

———. *Untitled (Black)*. 2005. Artist's collection. Santa Cruz, CA. Ink on petal and leaf paper, 5 in. x 5.5 in.

———. *Untitled (Exhaust)*. 2005. Artist's collection. Santa Cruz, CA. Ink and watercolor on paper, 9 in. x 12 in.

ABOUT THE AUTHOR

Ronaldo V. Wilson, PhD, is the author of *Narrative of the Life of the Brown Boy and the White Man* (University of Pittsburgh Press, 2008), winner of the 2007 Cave Canem Poetry Prize; *Poems of the Black Object* (Futurepoem Books, 2009), winner of the 2010 Asian American Literary Award and the Thom Gunn Award for Gay Poetry; and *Lucy 72* (1913 Press, 2015). He has held numerous fellowships, including the National Research Council Ford Foundation, The Fine Arts Work Center in Provincetown, Yaddo, Cave Canem, Kundiman, and Djerassi, and served as an Artist-in-Residence at the Headlands Center for the Arts, and the Center for Art and Thought (CA+T). Co-founder of the Black Took Collective, Wilson is currently an Associate Professor of Poetry, Fiction and Literature, and Core Faculty of the PhD Creative/Critical Concentration in the Literature Department at the University of California, Santa Cruz.